THE PSYCHODYNAMICS OF
SOCIAL NETWORKING

PSYCHOANALYSIS AND POPULAR CULTURE SERIES

Series Editors: Caroline Bainbridge and Candida Yates

Consulting Editor: Brett Kahr

Other titles in the Psychoanalysis and Popular Culture Series:

Television and Psychoanalysis: Psycho-Cultural Perspectives
  edited by Caroline Bainbridge, Ivan Ward, and Candida Yates

The Inner World of Doctor Who: Psychoanalytic Reflections in Time and Space
  by Iain MacRury and Michael Rustin

THE PSYCHODYNAMICS OF SOCIAL NETWORKING

Connected-up Instantaneous Culture and the Self

Aaron Balick

KARNAC

First published in 2014 by
Karnac Books Ltd
118 Finchley Road, London NW3 5HT

British Library Cataloguing in Publication Data

A C.I.P. for this book is available from the British Library

ISBN 978 1 78049 092 2

Edited, designed and produced by The Studio Publishing Services Ltd
www.publishingservicesuk.co.uk
e-mail: studio@publishingservicesuk.co.uk

Printed in Great Britain

www.karnacbooks.com

CONTENTS

ACKNOWLEDGEMENTS

Seeing this book from conception to completion has been a long process that has involved a great number of people. First and foremost, I would like to thank those directly involved in its coming into being. Brett Kahr, who first proposed the idea, and Caroline Bainbridge and Candida Yates, the series editors, who have given me the honour not only of being included in this exciting series, but also many other aspects of their prolific endeavours in psychoanalysis and culture. Those at Karnac Books who have so beneficently guided me through this process; Constance Govindin, Rod Tweedy, and Kate Pearce, who so helpfully and rapidly responded to my myriad e-mails, and Oliver Rathbone for taking this book on. I would also like to thank the journal *Psychoanalysis, Culture and Society* who first published my clinical paper "TMI in the transference LOL: Psychoanalytic reflections on Google, social networking, and 'virtual impingement'", which served as the basis for Chapter Two of this book. I am also eternally grateful to Alain Bartolo, a true and treasured friend, who was a constant source of encouragement and helpful criticism, and the first reader of so much of this book. Alain, *merci*. Further, this book would never have been possible were it not for my own client "Thomas", who was not only instrumental in helping me think through the implications of our own "virtual impingement" and all that followed, but generously gave consent for me to use his material in this book.

In writing a book there is a series of individuals who take on less formal roles that I would also like to thank. Foremost, I would like to thank two of my mentors, who have both "parented" me in deeply important ways in my development as a psychotherapist and writer, Andrew Samuels and Susie Orbach, both of whom have been pioneers in the application of the depth psychologies to society and culture. The executive board and members of the Relational School have all been there from the start, providing a fertile proving ground for this material, testing it, challenging it, and adding spice and content. I am grateful to the entire membership for their contribution and particularly the executive board; Shoshi Asheri, Sally Berry, Robert Downes, Jane Haberlin, Sue Jenssen, Pam Kleinot, Marsha Nodelman, Jane Nairne, and Judy Yellin. Also highly influential to me are my friends and colleagues at the Centre for Psychoanalytic Studies at the University of Essex, particularly Matt ffytche and Kevin Lu, alongside all the wonderful students who passed through our classes. I am also grateful to Ford Hickson for his help in my understanding of statistical and quantitative studies.

No book can be written without the love and support of those around you. On this point, the biggest acknowledgement goes out to my civil and life partner, Will Nutland, who, as part of his very being, effortlessly assuages my doubts, consistently settles my insecurities, and grounds me in the solid foundations of his love and affection. To Richard Kahwagi, not just for creating the beautiful cover, but also for his wonderfully accessible warmth, effervescent curiosity, humour, and relentless support. And to Juan Sanchez, whose quiet and patient belief in me has been profoundly sustaining.

I am deeply lucky to have a large family of origin and family of choice: too many to name. However, I would especially like to thank my mother, Leslie Balick Picker, and father, Stanley Balick, to whom I owe so much; my dear sister, Kheyala Rasa, and her two wonderful children, Ananda and Zack, who came back into my life during the writing of this book; and my stepfather, Lester Picker, who has been a great support. To my extended family, you know who you are, and to my family of choice all over the globe, I am most deeply grateful.

Permissions and copyrights

Epigraphs

Introduction:
Kranzberg, Melvin. Technology and history: 'Kranzberg's Laws'. *Technology and Culture*, 27(3) (1986): 545. © 1986 by the Society for the History of Technology. Reprinted with permission of the Johns Hopkins University Press.

Chapter Two:
Reprinted from *Hope and Dread in Psychoanalysis*, by Stephen A. Mitchell. Available from Basic Books, an imprint of Perseus Books Group. Copyright © 1983.

Chapter Three:
McLuhan, Marshall (1964). *Understanding Media*. New York: Routledge (2001), p. 52.

Chapter Four:
"Birdhouse in Your Soul", by John Linnell and John Flansburgh, Copyright © 1991 TMBG Music. All rights administered by Warner-Tamerlane Publishing Corp. All rights reserved. Used by permission.

Chapter Five:
Bollas, Christopher (1987). *Shadow of the Object*. Pages 48–49. © Christopher Bollas 1987. First published by Free Association Books, London, UK.

Throughout

Copyright © 2011 Sherry Turkle. Reprinted by permission of Basic Books, a member of Perseus Books Group.

To HB and TT
In memory of SWB

ABOUT THE AUTHOR

Aaron Balick is a UKCP registered psychotherapist and supervisor, and a media and social networking consultant working in London. He is also an honorary lecturer at the Centre for Psychoanalytic Studies at the University of Essex, where he participates in the postgraduate MA and PhD programmes in psychoanalytic studies; in addition, he lectures and runs workshops in a variety of psychotherapy trainings in the UK. As a founding and executive member of the Relational School UK, he works to develop and promote relational thinking in the UK and abroad. Dr Balick writes for both academic and lay audiences, having published several academic articles and book chapters, while at the same time contributing a psychological angle in the national press and on national radio; he has also written a self-help book for children. He is a media spokesperson for the UKCP and a regular contributor, as the "resident psychotherapist", to BBC Radio 1's phone-in show, *The Surgery with Aled and Dr Radha*.

The application of psychoanalytic ideas and theories to culture has a long tradition and this is especially the case with cultural artefacts that might be considered "classical" in some way. For Sigmund Freud, the works of William Shakespeare and Johann Wolfgang von Goethe were as instrumental as those of culturally renowned poets and philosophers of classical civilisation in helping to formulate the key ideas underpinning psychoanalysis as a psychological method. In the academic fields of the humanities and social sciences, the application of psychoanalysis as a means of illuminating the complexities of identity and subjectivity is now well established. However, despite these developments, there is relatively little work that attempts to grapple with popular culture in its manifold forms, some of which, nevertheless, reveal important insights into the vicissitudes of the human condition.

The "Psychoanalysis and Popular Culture" book series builds on the work done since 2009 by the Media and the Inner World research network, which was generously funded by the UK's Arts and Humanities Research Council. It aims to offer spaces to consider the relationship between psychoanalysis in all its forms and popular culture, which is ever more emotionalised in the contemporary age.

In contrast to many scholarly applications of psychoanalysis, which often focus solely on "textual analysis", this series sets out to explore the creative tension of thinking about cultural experience and its processes, with attention to observations from the clinical and scholarly fields of observation. What can academic studies drawing on psychoanalysis learn from the clinical perspective and how might the critical insights afforded by scholarly work cast new light on clinical experience? The series provides space for a dialogue between these different groups with a view to creating fresh perspectives on the values and pitfalls of a psychoanalytic approach to ideas of selfhood, society, and popular culture. In particular, the series strives to develop a psycho-cultural approach to such questions by drawing attention to the usefulness of a post-Freudian, object-relations perspective for examining the importance of emotional relationships and experience.

The Psychodynamics of Social Networking: Connected-up Instantaneous Culture and the Self addresses these themes of the series by placing psychoanalytic understandings of selfhood, relatedness, and popular culture at its core. The author, Aaron Balick, draws on his expertise in clinical, academic, and media fields to explore the experiential processes of social media and their role in shaping subjectivity in the settings and contexts of everyday life. The book examines the dynamic interplay between the socio-cultural forces and technological developments that have facilitated new ways of relating and communicating with one another, creating spaces for the psycho-cultural imagination, where the fantasy life of object relating can take place. Balick first explored some of these themes and ideas in public roundtable and workshop discussions organised by the Media and Inner World research network, and the editors of this series are very pleased that this association has proved to be so fruitful. (For further details of that activity, see: www.miwnet.org.) This book builds on some of that work and provides a highly innovative, psychodynamic perspective on the experience of social networking and its dilemmas for the subject of the contemporary mediatised age.

Caroline Bainbridge and Candida Yates
Series Editors

Introduction: putting it into context

"Technology is neither good nor bad; nor is it neutral"

(Kranzberg's First Law of Technology, 1986)

Given the rapidly evolving nature of the world of online social networking, this book knowingly works within the risk that things will have surely changed even by the time the binding glue cools as it comes off the presses. The pace of change in today's new media and mobile technology is such that as soon as words go on to a page in relation to them, they are at risk of becoming out-dated by the time the ink has dried. Maybe you are reading this as an e-book, in which case the idea of the ink drying and an actual paper binding already seems anachronistic. In my research for this book, I came across many examples of "the next big thing" that the tech gurus predicted would come to define our culture for the next decade; most of these were flashes in the pan, trends that disappeared as quickly as they appeared. Even the notion of "defining a decade" is changing—a decade is too long and things are changing too quickly. Just think of the rapid rise of MySpace or Second Life, both of which captured the cultural imagination only to be rendered practically obsolete eighteen to twenty-four months later. One by one these entities burst on to the scene only to wither on the vine, to be replaced by new iterations of online social experiences. I have learnt a great deal by reading about their rapid rises and slightly more protracted near demises; you see, they never seem to die: they simply revert into rarefied social niches with cult audiences. In order to future-proof this text as much as possible, I have chosen to take a process-orientated approach rather than a content-orientated one. While a content-orientated approach would be primarily interested in examining social networking sites (SNSs) as they currently exist, the alternative process-orientated approach will focus instead on the *processes* in which individuals and our society at large are implicated and mediated within online social media itself. Hence, the use of the word "psychodynamics" in the title should alert you that it is the dynamics (the forces behind) that will be the locus of interest, not the object itself. Psychodynamics is utilised as an umbrella term to identify a whole series of theories and practices developed through the various schools of psychoanalysis that investigate human motivation, meaning-making, and unconscious process. Because SNSs are likely to continue to develop rapidly in as yet unexpected ways, the question of how humans might psychologically adapt to these rapid changes remains open. Naughton (2012a) notes that disruption and change is essential to the Internet as a whole, not just social networking. For Naughton, the Internet

> is a global machine for springing surprises—good, bad, and indifferent—on us. What's more, it was explicitly designed to be like this, though its designers might not have expressed it in precisely those terms. In other words, the disruptiveness of the Internet is a *feature*, not a bug—it stems from the basic architectural principles of the network's design. It's what the network was designed to do. So you could say that disruptiveness is built into its virtual DNA. (p. 33)

The way in which the disruptive nature of online technology operates alongside the ways that social media mediates the basic human dynamics of relating will consistently be the centre of interest of this text; this model should continue to be amenable to application to as yet unanticipated iterations of social networking. We will keep coming back to the question of where and how virtual DNA meets human psychological DNA; how the contemporary mode of digital expression meets our deepest unconscious need to recognise, be recognised, and relate to others: our psychodynamics.

A very short history of online social networks

Online social networking has penetrated our social landscape, saturating our methods of relating with profound speed and accelerating growth. This has been made possible by the social shaping of technology (see Chapter Three), that is, the interplay of socio-cultural forces and technological development that has enabled technology to more readily meet the needs of the non-specialist population, a process exemplified in the enormous success and popularity of Facebook. The speed at which Facebook has become the world's most popular and ubiquitous SNS is unprecedented. On 4 October 2012, Mark Zuckerberg announced that Facebook had one billion active accounts (Facebook, 2012a); it is estimated that thirty-eight per cent of Internet users throughout the world are active on Facebook (Solis, 2012). With a world population of around seven billion, Facebook represents 12% of it; if Facebook were a nation, it would be the third largest in the world (Solis, 2012). At present, Facebook is the second most visited site in the world after Google (Fitzgerald, 2012). Setting the context for how this became so can begin to give us an idea about what kind of psychological role the modern online social network is providing for its everyday users.

It was a series of failures and half-starts that paved the way for Facebook's dominance. Facebook is merely the most recent and dominant iteration of SNSs that developed out of smaller projects explicitly aimed at connecting people in new ways. It is no accident that the same telephone lines that have connected people for the previous century have become the conduit for the next generation of technological connection. Alas, the lowly telephone line proved itself too slow for the increasing demand for speed; across the connected-up world, old copper telephone lines are being ripped out and replaced by faster fibre-optic cables. Expansion of Internet use has been exceptional, resulting in the developments of what has been termed "Web 2.0" (Creeber & Martin, 2009), that is, the shifting of the World Wide Web from being dominated by static content-heavy web pages to becoming more interactive and explicitly social. Naughton (2012a) describes Web 1.0 as "a world-wide repository of linked, static documents held on servers distributed across the Internet" (p. 134). The main driver behind the shift to Web 2.0 was e-commerce, "which desperately needed to transform the Web into a medium that facilitated *transactions*" (p. 136). Although Naughton is referring to financial transactions, the same motivation that enabled their development also facilitated the ease of human-to-human *interactions*. This move towards interaction is largely responsible for shifting focus from a content-focused platform to one that relies upon user engagement; in this sense, you can see the development of Web 2.0 as a relational process itself, one that has been inexorably moving towards a connected-up, instantaneous culture. Although Web 2.0 continues to be content-heavy, it is the nature of the social networking *process* that has arguably drawn the Internet into the lives of everyday people. However, it was not always thus.

In the simplest terms, the Internet[1] was developed as the most expedient way to send and receive information. In order to do this in the best possible way, it was based on two rules; that there should be no central control and that it should be simple, that is, not optimised for any single application (Naughton, 2012a, p. 186), which is why it is just as easy to send video, text, voice, images, or anything else from point A to point B. According to Wikipedia, the word "Internet" with a capital "I" is meant to indicate the Internet that we use every day, distinguishing it from internets in general, which can refer to any connected online network. The Web (or World Wide Web) is the series of networked "pages" that we use to interface across the Internet (but it is not *the* Internet), whereas SNSs are the parts of the Web upon which we use social networking. The distinctions are important. While the Internet itself developed earlier than the social web that carries our SNSs, today's SNSs developed atop this infrastructure, emerging from their less "user friendly" forebears during the infancy of the World Wide Web, developing explicitly with the aim of connecting people.

Early adopters will be familiar with the Internet bulletin boards systems (BBSs) that emerged in the 1980s across the aforementioned clunky modems in which telephone receivers sat like birds in nests. Those who forged the earliest social networks were not seen as pioneers at the time by their social network-naïve public, rather, they were often seen as feckless and antisocial "computer nerds". They were, however, relating to other people the whole time, only through the medium of a computer-mediated network pioneering a completely new way of online relating that would revolutionise our social world. It was these early hobbyists that forged ahead with the more user friendly interfaces that would, in later years of the first decade of the twenty-first century, be utilised by hundreds of millions of people who would not know what a "baud"[2] rate was if it hit them in the face, or be familiar with the screeching noise that used to accompany every online connection. These informal BBS networks (usually hosted on a computer hobbyist's home server) were followed by commercial ventures, now mostly forgotten, such as Prodigy and, later, AOL (America On Line), which continues today in a different form; these packages made it easier for those who were not serious computer hobbyists to join the fun—and it soon caught on. The growing ubiquity of email to the general public from the early 1990s ensured that more and more people were wired in, if not yet connected to the growing World Wide Web that was hurtling toward 2.0. Each development produced a new human-to-machine interface that became more intuitive and more human with each iteration: the development of the web browser being a prime example of this process. This is the social shaping hypothesis (Baym, 2010) in action: technology meets human desire, and then by way of human innovation, the technology adapts to better meet these desires. Gone are clunky monochrome screens and indecipherable DOS commands; welcome the intuitive touch screen you can put in your pocket and a colourful human interface with all the creepy architecture well hidden in the background. This is, of course, a double-edged sword. We have accepted the ease of the interface at the expense of not understanding how these technologies operate, and that has grave consequences, many of which we have yet to fully comprehend.

Off the back of these rather clunky BBSs, SNSs had a few incarnations before becoming mainstream, including Six Degrees as early as 1997 and Friendster in 2002 (boyd & Ellison, 2007). Growth became exponential, particularly with the development of Myspace, which launched in 2004. Myspace started to attract large numbers of participants, gaining a million subscribers in its first month of operation in February of 2004, growing to five million by November of the same year; by 2005, the BBC reported that it was the most viewed internet domain in the USA (Stenovec, 2011). The first indications of the scope and range of the SNS was now becoming apparent. Although Myspace never achieved the ubiquity that Facebook would, it was, none the less, the first social network to really become a household word as well as being the first online public venue through which our culture would first come across the notion of cyberbullying and cyberstalking: the instant fame that the Internet made possible, and the "go-to place" for journalists to more easily find photographs and material on individuals involved in political scandals and other head-line-grabbing news. While Myspace was still largely the preserve of the young, and in many ways the hip music-aware young, the idea of the online social network started becoming part of the cultural consciousness across the social spectrum. Facebook opened up to the wider public in 2006, two years after Myspace, though its popularity soared, taking over Myspace's 75.9 million subscribers a mere two years later (Stenovec, 2011). Just four years after that, Facebook's online population reached half a billion (Facebook, 2011), before doubling two years after that. These statistics are important to note, as they indicate the vast number of individuals motivated to visit these sites: further, they exemplify in pure quantitative terms that moving towards online social networking is *catchy*, once a critical mass of individuals comes on board, they attract more and more, ultimately making this form of relating mainstream. Put in the perspective of *mainstream relating*, we can see the draw: Facebook and other SNSs are tools that we use to relate to others; as this text will draw out, the motivation to relate to others is one of the most profound drives that lie at the centre of what it means to be human. The way in which SNSs seek to harness the massive power of this motivation is one of the main attractions it has to investors and marketers who are constantly seeking out ways to capitalise on them. The potentially psychodynamic consequences of this drive towards capitalisation, as exemplified in Facebook becoming a publically traded company in 2012, will be discussed in Chapter Four.

Facebook was not initially successful in monetising its operation, experiencing a serious drop in its share price shortly after its initial public offering (IPO); struggling until the summer of 2013 to recover to near its offer price; we can expect continued volitility. Perhaps one of the reasons why the users of Facebook have initially seemed reluctant to turn a profit for those that run it may have to do with the nature of what an online social network actually is, and what fundamentally motivates it to grow. Its main attraction appears to be its ability to create an environment for people to connect to each other, rather than to shop, much to the consternation of those trying desperately to exploit this paradigm better for this purpose. But what is it that explicitly defines a social networking site? Throughout this text, I will be using boyd and Ellison's (2007) definition of the SNS:

We define social network sites as web-based services that allow individuals to (1) construct a public or semi-public profile within a bounded system, (2) articulate a list of other users with whom they share a connection, and (3) view and traverse their list of connections and those made by others within the system.

To this, I would add other staples of modern-day SNSs, such as the ability to comment upon and share information, post photos, and a whole variety of other activities that are primarily based on sharing things with others across an online network. These elements seem to operate as an underlying architecture among the variety of social networks that come and go. In addition to traditional online social networks such as Facebook and Twitter, there is a plethora of other online platforms that contain social elements, such as Internet gaming, Internet dating sites, and virtual worlds like Second Life, a variety of social applications such as Instagram (sharing photographs) and Foursquare (sharing venues with friends such as restaurants and bars), smartphone applications for finding instant sexual gratification like Grindr and Blendr, and other platforms all together, such as YouTube and Vine for sharing videos. While all of these are important loci of online human experience and psychosocial research, they cannot possibly all be investigated in depth in this text.

Google search, while not a traditional online social network, is the most visited site on the Internet (Alexa, 2012) and although it is mostly associated with searching for information about *stuff*, Chapter Two will look at it in the context in which it is often used to seek information about *other people and ourselves*; rather than being a simple source of data, the information collected about individual persons on Google's knowledge graph has psychological consequences for the way we see ourselves and others. That Google is also under investigation in this text necessarily opens up the set of technological platforms that can be considered as domains of online social relating worthy of interest: these include mobile technologies such as smartphones and tablets (Chapter Three) and other online interactional environments, such as comment pages on news sites (Chapter Four), alongside a whole variety of other online spaces that enable online interpersonal relating. While the main focus for this book will be on the function that SNSs have as a virtual site of person-to-person relating and its nature as a primary medium through which this is currently taking place, other domains of interpersonal relating will come in when appropriate.

Why psychodynamic?

As the title of this book clearly suggests, the theoretical underpinning of this text will be psychodynamic. While Chapter One will draw out the details of what I call a relational psychodynamic approach, at this stage it is important to simply note that "psychodynamic" is an inclusive umbrella term for a range of theories and therapeutic practices that developed out of psychoanalysis and take the nature of the dynamic unconscious as a central tenet of its worldview. There are many schools of psychoanalysis (from Adler to Žižek) that share a common ancestry back to Freud, although to this day the field remains "schoolist" and divided. Therefore, the word *psychodynamic* is used as an inclusive term that allows for the insights of a variety of these schools to be applied to our object of investigation, allowing a flexible and less dogmatic approach to the material at hand. While left intentionally broad, my use of the term is bound together by guiding principles outlined by Jacobs (1998), in which the essence of psychodynamic theory lies in three domains: first, conceptual modelling, which is derived from the clinical situation and therapeutic relationship through which the understanding of the patient's unconscious relational dynamics are laid bare by "working through defences and resistance, as well as the use of transference and counter-transference" (p. 1); second, from the theoretical perspective, with regard to models of human development, "how people develop through childhood and through adolescence into adult life; and what this process imparts to them along the way" (p. 2); third, a comprehensive mapping of personality structure, "models of how the mind works, or of how the personality might be structured" (p. 5). Each of these domains rests upon a fundamental acceptance of a dynamic unconscious that underlies each of them. While these main themes inform the broad psychodynamic approach, more precise terms will be brought in from individual traditions of psychoanalysis when appropriate.

Given that we are investigating a thoroughly contemporary paradigm that is both fast-moving and embedded within the technological world, it is fair to ask why a discipline that was developed in the nineteenth century and originally required nothing more than a couch and a chair is an appropriate lens through which to view this highly modern technological phenomena. While, on the one hand, one might argue that psychoanalysis is an outdated and anachronistic model with which to approach cutting edge modernity in the form of online social networking, on the other hand, we can clearly see that a psychoanalytic perspective includes models of unconscious motivation, identity development, and a theory of relational structures that allows us to approach social networking with a depth that might not be readily available from other methods. These models, rather than having been preserved in Victorian aspic, have undergone well over a century of working through and revision, resulting in a modern iteration of psychoanalysis that has not only undergone changes within its own paradigm, but also allowed itself to be influenced by a variety of social and cultural disciplines, including sociology, feminism, critical theory, postmodernism, and the observational and empirical sciences, from attachment studies to fMRI scans in neuroscience.

Relational psychoanalysis, which will be discussed in detail in Chapter One, is considered a development of the object relations tradition, as hinted at in Freud's late writings and developed by Klein, Fairbairn, Winnicott, and others (Mitchell & Greenberg, 1983). Object relations theory shifted the focus from libido as a pleasure seeking energy requiring release to the new paradigm of the libido as object-seeking[3] instead, in which "[t]he fundamental motivational push in human experience is not gratification and tension reduction, using others as a means toward that end, but connections with others as an end in itself" (Mitchell & Black, 1995, p. 115). The nature of this motivation resulted in the images of other people, or parts or aspects of other people (referred to as "objects") taking up residency in the individual subject as internal objects. Paraphrasing Fairbairn, Mitchell and Black (1995) describe people as, "actually structured into multiple, subtly discontinuous self organizations, different versions of ourselves with particular different characteristics" (p. 121); these versions of ourselves are directly related to our internalisations of others. While object relations was a great advance, it suffered from reducing others to "objects" in the mind of the subject under study, rather than as subjects in relation to other subjects. British psychoanalyst Donald

Winnicott can, in many ways, be retrospectively seen as "relational" because he shifted focus again toward a more intersubjective angle on the infant–mother relationship. Although his insights were focused primarily on the perspective of the infant's internal world, he deviated from the object relations tradition as associated with Klein and Fairbairn by noting that the nature of the facilitating environment provided by the "good enough" mother was essential in healthy psychological development. This change recognised the importance of others in the subject's own psychological development.

This move towards intersubjectivity and the nature of objects *vs.* subjects became the key change that developed into relational psychoanalysis, originally inspired by Mitchell and Greenberg (1983) and further developed by Mitchell (1988, 1993), Benjamin (1988, 1995) Aron (1996), and a raft of others found in the edited compilations of papers by Mitchell and Aron (1999) and Aron and Harris (2005). Contemporary psychoanalysis has been influenced by all of these developments, enabling a contemporary post-Freudian psychoanalysis to develop a creative alternative to its predecessors and make it possible to address developments in our modern twenty-first century culture from a refreshed psychodynamic perspective. The nature of SNSs is fundamentally relational and calls upon its users to interact with them through both their internal object relations and intersubjective engagements with others; relational psychoanalysis offers a series of models to understand these processes. Therefore, two positions will be axiomatic throughout this text: first, that the primary motivation that lies at the bottom of people's social networking use is relational in nature. Second, that by taking a process-orientated approach to social networking use, we can gain a foothold into the meanings that these relational motivations hold for individuals through the mediation and architecture of the online social network. Following on from these axioms, it seems clear that a multi-disciplinary approach, broadly housed under the title *psychosocial*, offers us the necessary theories and concepts to apply to this material in a grounded and flexible, yet critical, fashion. It is necessary that the *psycho* here is indicative of contemporary psychoanalysis rather than the field of experimental psychology, which is so much better represented in the field of social networking research.

Social networking is individual, intersubjective, and social:
it is also commercial and potentially objectifying

While a broadly psychosocial and phenomenological approach seems an obvious avenue into the online social networking phenomenon, it is hardly surprising that the bulk of the material I encountered in preparation for this book came not from psychoanalysis, but, rather, from the world of commerce, in particular the marketing and branding sectors of industry that are producing reams of material focused on customer engagement (with products and brands) and the use of social media as an engine of person-to-person "informal" advertising: an application within social media that is on the verge of creating vast amounts of money. Because of this, a great deal of research has been going into how best to capitalise on the vast stores of personal information collected by SNSs of their users, and rather less on trying to understand how users *make meaning* of their SNS activity (something that is unlikely to produce a financial return). The writing of this book overlapped with the IPO of Facebook, launching with a headline-grabbing value of over 100 billion US dollars, making it an opening day record for a technology company and the third largest IPO ever launched on the New York Stock Exchange (Pepitone, 2012). Shortly after its launch, Facebook shares lost a substantial amount of value as a result of both financial irregularities in relation to the IPO itself and continued doubts about how Facebook might be able to monetise its vast resources, particularly on mobile phones that have little room for advertising space. The enormous size of the initial financial investment Facebook's IPO attracted, alongside continued interest in its highly volatile share price, indicates the value that commercial entities and investors are placing on Facebook's potential to understand people's social networking habits in the name of profit. The collection of these habits as a whole is considered a resource of great value and the exploitation of this resource is referred to as "data mining". The virtual world has become the site of the next "gold rush", a land full of data mines where speculators flock to exploit their potential value.

In the early days of the Internet during Web 1.0, brands hoping to exploit the web for commerce frequently repeated the mantra that "content is king", a phrase meant to indicate that marketers needed to prioritise their thinking on the online *content* they provided in order to promote their brand, maximise interest in their products (by encouraging people to their websites), and, ultimately, increase their sales. This focus on content is related to the nature of the Web 1.0 itself because of the static characteristics of its infrastructure. More recently, with the development of Web 2.0, the key idea has shifted from "content" to "engagement", a shift that acknowledges that providing good content is no longer enough: advertisers must now engage their customers not only with their products, but with each other *about* their products. This shift, in many ways, can be seen as analogous to the shift in psychoanalytic theory from object relations to relational psychoanalysis: a move from a subject relating to objects to subjects relating to other subjects, in this case, across a digital network. The shift of focus to engagement from content seems to indicate that those who wish to utilise social media for commercial gain are seeking to exploit the primary human motivation to relate to others for their commercial purposes: a human motivation that psychoanalysis has been occupied with for well over 100 years. Just think of how early advertisers relied on Freud's findings with regard to sexuality by using sex to sell products. Today's advertisers appear to be keeping up with developments in psychoanalysis and have moved on from using just sex to sell towards using personal relationships to do exactly the same thing. Just as relational psychoanalysis sits on top of its forbears in a holistic way by being inclusive of earlier theories that are still seen to bring value, advertisers, too, have not dropped using sex to sell, they have just added relationships to their toolboxes.

Psychoanalysis has always preferred to focus on underlying process, looking into the fundamentals of psychological *engagement* rather than being consumed solely with the narrative content. For a psychoanalyst, it is a novice's error to be "taken in" by content at the expense of process; a patient's *narrative content* is not quite as important as the way in which that narrative is deployed in the consulting room by way of their process (transference, projection, etc.). The analyst asks not only what the patient is saying, but at the same time enquires into the way in which they are "engaged" in the therapeutic relationship. The analyst is not just looking for the narrative that is being consciously communicated, but also what is being communicated unconsciously, communications that also effect change in the other. Freud (1915e) notes, "it is a very remarkable thing that the *Ucs* [system unconscious] of one human being can react upon that of another" (p. 194). Outside the clinic (and online) these unconscious communications are part and parcel of human relating: within the consultation room, it is *the very object of interest*. The analyst uses herself in a particular way to receive the unconscious intersubjective communications from the patient; she then assimilates it and delivers it back, enabling the patient to make it conscious for himself. Interestingly, for our purposes, Freud (1912e) offers the metaphor of the telephone in helping us to understand how unconscious-to-unconscious communication operates:

> [the analyst] must turn his unconscious like a receptive organ towards the transmitting unconscious of the patient. He must adjust himself to the patient as a telephone is adjusted to the transmitting microphone. Just as the receiver converts back into sound wave the electronic oscillations in the telephone line which were set up by sound waves, so the doctor's unconscious is able, from the derivatives of the unconscious which are communicated to him, to reconstruct that unconscious, which was delivered by the patient's free associations. (pp. 115–116)

While the content of the narrative remains an important aspect of the analysis, it is the unconscious motivation and relational dynamics that interests the psychoanalyst and the "working through" of that motivation that ultimately moves the therapy on. To carry on Freud's metaphor, the words that are conveyed over the telephone are important, but it is the intention behind the words and why those words are deployed that carry a further and more profound meaning. By understanding the process—the desire and motivations behind social networking—do we really access not just the "what" but the "why" of social networking? It seems to me that the vast amount of resources that are currently going into working out how to utilise social networking data for commercial advantage is being developed at the expense of using some of the same resources to enable us to understand people better. Most worrying about this trajectory is the amount of energy going into fostering brand loyalty among young people at the expense of understanding young people themselves. Fortunately, some researchers (e.g., Clarke (2009), boyd (2008), Turkle (2011), and others) are doing some very exciting work in seeking to understand engagement with SNSs beyond basic commercial aims. It is also worth noting that the bulk of non-commercial psychological research into social networking is not concerned with the meaning-making that has so interested psychodynamic therapists, but, rather, large-scale studies of groups (frequently university undergraduates) to learn about how online time is allocated, or to find correlations between personality and social networking use. Where relevant, these studies will be included and read with a psychodynamic eye.

Methodology: applied psychoanalysis

By applying principles of psychodynamic theory, I will be provoking some questions about the processes that underlie the unconscious motivations behind the way individuals engage with SNSs, that is, the nature of what goes on *in between* the individual and the online social network itself, as well as that which goes on *in between those individuals engaged with each other* as mediated by the social network. Turkle (2011) opens her excellent book, *Alone Together: Why We Expect More from Technology and Less from Each Other*, with a rather pithy, profound quote, "Technology proposes itself as the architect of our intimacies" (p. 1). This statement naturally provokes inquiries into the nature of this architect, and how its mediation affects our intimate lives. Language has long been the architect of our intimacies, and the written word a tool of that architect. What technology has proposed itself more as an architect to our intimacies than the love letter? Today, how many young people receive their first love letter not on scented wax-sealed paper, but, rather, in the form of a message over Facebook chat, or a text on their mobile phone? Heartbreakingly, how many intimate relationships are finished by way of text message or email? Social media and other social technologies, such as those embedded in smartphones, have become the new technologies of our intimacies. In order to gain some purchase on the ways in which this technology both mediates and structures our intimate and not-so-intimate inter-actions, I will be applying psychodynamic theory in reading both existing (non-psychoanalytic) research and analyses of publicly avail-able cultural artefacts, such as news articles, blogs, and media com-mentary. My approach in this text is not a comprehensive study in its own right, but, rather, a thematic and psychodynamic interpretation of the materials I have come across in researching this book.

Both relational psychoanalysis and contemporary qualitative psychosocial research methodologies require a degree of reflexivity from the clinician or researcher. For both disciplines, this reflexivity acknowledges the subjectivity of the analyst or researcher in the hope that biases will be honestly apprehended while also acknowledging that the presence of a human subject, be it a psychoanalyst or a researcher, affects their patient in analysis or, indeed, those individuals or groups of individuals who are the subjects of research. In the spirit of this reflexivity, I wish to declare that during the writing of this book I have embedded myself in social media and have relied heavily on it to acquire much of the data I have chosen to analyse. For example, when I began to write this book I reluctantly set up a Twitter account to "follow" many leading thinkers in the field and, through this account, I have managed to collect a great deal of material to analyse. Many people who have no experience of Twitter are unaware that more than simply supplying snippets or fragments of minutiae, tweets can contain links to research papers, blogs, articles, and a whole raft of information, given that one takes care to follow the appropriate people. My personal engagement in SNSs, and particularly Twitter and Facebook, have given me a different perspective compared to what I have frequently found to be a knee-jerk suspicion in the psychoanalytic community about these platforms. Seligman (2011), for example, states,

> Web 2.0 seems to take what used to be called the 'sound bite' to a new extreme, implying that you can represent yourself with a few words and images and describe your status in a phrase that you can change with a few keystrokes . . . or communicate what's going on at the moment in 147 [sic] characters or less. [p. 504]

With all due respect to Seligman, I have some doubts that he has engaged across these platforms well enough to really know this to be true. If he had, he would know that statuses are social and interactive in nature and, as we shall see in this text, usually regulated and interacted with by known others. Second, he would have known that while Twitter may be used to communicate what is going on in a moment (140 characters or less, not 147) it is also a multi-media platform in which individuals communicate with others, share links to important papers, make requests and have them kindly answered, among a whole variety of other potential *interpersonal and social* experiences. Without wholly putting oneself into the experience, it may be difficult to fully understand it. Furthermore, as many psychoanalytic writers are theorising from the position of their patients' problematic relationships with the virtual world, their opinions on the nature of the paradigm as a whole may be somewhat skewed towards pathological modelling

In addition to my Twitter profile, I also set up a public Facebook page on social media research to collect both information and stories about people's social networking use, though this has been far less successful[4] and of less use to me than Twitter. Probably partly due to this book, my own personal use of SNSs has increased, even though I came to social networking rather later than many of those in my "real world" social network, creating my first SNS profile (a private Facebook page) at the end of March 2007 (or so my Facebook timeline tells me). My previously casual engagement with social networking has become clearly more intensive, something about which I have been forced to become reflective. After the purchase of a smartphone, my use of Twitter increased a great deal, at times approaching an intensity of interest analogous to a compulsive quality. I have been mindful of my own SNS use across the period of writing this book and have kept process notes about it. Because of this experience, it might be said that this research is somewhat ethnographic, and that I have "gone native". An ethnographic approach is one that has a focus on

> an entire cultural group . . . typically it is large, involving many people who interact over time . . . Ethnography is a qualitative design in which the researcher describes and interprets the shared and learned patterns of values, behaviours, beliefs and language of a culture-sharing group. (Creswell, 2007, p. 68)

Traditional ethnographies are complex affairs and conducting ethnography online brings with it its own set of problems. Kozinets (2010), however, notes that desire to produce a "real" or "authentic" ethnography is a misguided one. For Kozinets, ethnography is always culturally contingent, "there is no *really real* ethnography, no *de facto* ethnography, no *de facto* perfect ethnography that would satisfy every methodological purist" (p. 62). This text does not purport to be a traditional ethnography, but, as will be expanded upon in Chapter One, it does use insights from the ethnographic tradition to help understand what I believe to be happening across SNSs. After all, the inspiration for writing this book emerged not from my engagement in SNSs, but through a clinical experience I had that was provoked by a Google search that will be discussed in detail in Chapter Two. Until the moment that the Google search became clinically relevant, I had not considered the platform to be replete with psychological meaning, although I found to my surprise that it was. I have come to see that some of the basic elements I discovered in coming to understand the psychological meaning inherent in my clinical experience with Google are equally implicated in SNSs, as they, too, are embedded in our culture. It is the nature of the psychological role that this embeddedness enables in our culture that will be the focus of this book.

It's more about the why than the what

Above, I asked why a discipline that emerged in the nineteenth century might be helpful to us in our thoroughly modern age of intense technological change. Turkle (2004) notes that it is fashionable to see the start of the new millennium as the end of the Freudian century and the start of the computer culture; this, she argues, is wrong:

> We must cultivate the richest possible language and methodologies for talking about our increasingly emotional relationships with [interactive digital] artefacts. We need far closer examination of how artefacts enter the development of self and mediate between self and other. Psychoanalysis provides a rich language for distinguishing between need (something that artefacts may have) and desire (which resides in the conjunction of language and flesh). It provides a rich language for exploring the specificity of human meanings in their connection to the body. (p. 29)

One of the primary dynamics I will be investigating throughout this text is the role that social networking has in the way contemporary users come to understand themselves and others through the media of online social networking: I wish to use the rich language of psychoanalysis to do so. Underlying the entire text will be the question that everyone seems to be asking these days: "Is the development of what has come to be called 'Web 2.0' and similar technologies (such as smartphones and tablets) changing us in some fundamental way, or are they simply novel technological platforms through which the same old psychological traits express themselves through a different medium?"

Although this is a question that it may be too early to answer with confidence, indications do seem to be leaning towards the "yes it is changing us" side of the equation. Naughton (2012a), reflecting on his two and a half decades of writing, thinking, and lecturing on the Internet, notes that

> our society has become critically dependent on a technology that is poorly understood, not just by its users, but also by people (like government ministers) who are in a position to make decisions about how it should be regulated and controlled. (pp. 10–11)

Morozov (2011) has a similar concern,

> The Internet does matter, but we simply don't know how it matters. This fact, paradoxically, only makes it matter even more: The costs of getting it wrong are tremendous . . . [the Internet] can never be really understood outside the context in which it manifests itself. (p. 30)

Engaging deeply within the context of the Internet with regard to social networking and the meta-phenomena that come with it is a stated aim of this book. The question of the empirical effects that SNSs, the Internet, and other technologies in general have on our brains and behaviour are currently being widely undertaken. Although these studies will not be the central focus of this text, such findings will be addressed where relevant. Those studies that do look at brain response and behaviour have emerged in response to the ubiquitous nature of online engagement that is unprecedented among both adults and young people. There is undoubtedly something very compelling about social networking that is simply evidenced in the fact that it has achieved the rapid growth and population penetration that we see today. When a psychoanalyst thinks about "something compelling", as a rule she is likely to be thinking about motivation: that which unconsciously compels. Whether referring back to Freud's notion of "libido" or "drive," Fairbairn's "object seeking", or Bowlby's interest in "attachment", all are concerned with what unconsciously motivates human desire and behaviour and, secondarily, the meaning-making that is built atop these same unconscious motivations. The details of this more precise conceptual approach will be covered in Chapter One, as will the details of the nature of such an application of these concepts outside the clinical situation. The transfer of psychodynamic applications from within the clinical situation to outside of it is an important development in researching social systems; the functioning and understanding of the intersubjective relationship as it is enacted unconsciously is central to both clinical psychotherapy and social research. In this sense my psychodynamic approach is essentially relational in nature, guided by the principle *that human motivation is profoundly relational in nature*: that our need to relate to one another is fundamental.

From the relational perspective, relating to each other is not just what motivates us from birth, but it continues to be the site of our challenges, pathologies, repetitions, and delights throughout the rest of our lives. Our histories strongly influence the ways in which we relate to each other in adult life, and relating to each other (whether with families, lovers, colleagues, or friends, or, more recently, our "friends" on Facebook or "followers" on Twitter) can both challenge and satisfy us like nothing else. The recent development of the social network which offers new technologies through which relating is mediated is a vast new world in which the way we make meaning of our relationships can be explored.

When we consider the compound term "social networking" itself, we can see that its construction contains both the basic elements of relating and technology; the technology is the "network" and the social is the human motivation that deploys the technology to this end. We are using the technology as a medium to relate, and that is why psychoanalysis can be utilised to understand the underlying processes informing this relating, and the potential consequences of it: both positive and negative. These consequences include the changing nature of privacy, the evolving concept of a "friend", the functioning of our online reputations and the permanence of our data trails, the ease and instantaneous nature of our communications across vast distances, the ease, too, of the replicability of anything that goes online, the lack of human-to-human feedback in contemporary online conversations (e.g., our growing reliance on text messaging, SNS posting, and Microsoft messaging (MSM) or Blackberry data services), among many others. Each of these "natures" are separate, though they operate alongside each other, overlapping and eventually multiplying the effects synergistically, resulting in a series of complex effects on our expectations, communication styles, relational styles, and even our identities. While the consequences of each technological medium has a different effect on us (e.g., Twitter tends to offer quicker, more immediate experience than Facebook), all of these media exist in a soup of "always on" potentialities, and it is the immersion within this soup that will also be addressed.

I will not delay offering conclusions until the end. By stating them up front it will be easier to demonstrate the thesis throughout: that the underlying motivation to relate (online and in "real life") is the desire for recognition. As we will see in Chapter One, this is already an axiomatic position that relational psychoanalysis has come to take in its understanding of both the psychoanalytic clinical endeavour and its application in other fields. The variety of recognition that is sought, however, is what might be called "authentic recognition", and there are a series of developmental obstacles affecting the ability both to accept and to give such recognition. I suggest here that the medium of online relating complicates this process even further.

The core angle from which I write this text is as a psychotherapist who, in his daily life, in both the consulting room and outside of it, has encountered the dynamics of social networking as they affect my clients, those around me, and myself. While those in my field have historically taken a case history methodology (Midgely, 2006), with the exception of the small case vignette in Chapter Two, I will not be taking such an approach, both for issues of confidentiality, and the nature of the possibility of skewing the findings towards a pathological angle, as noted above. While a case study approach may still be helpful for mental health clinicians working with individuals who are having a problematic relationship with the Internet, and social networking in particular, my goal in this text is a broader one: that is, to utilise the insight that a psychodynamic approach can provide and apply it to culture outside the consulting room. While the language I use may be clinically derived, this is not a text about the clinical "treatment" of disorders associated with the online world. It was, indeed, the event that occurred within my own consulting room that I describe in Chapter Two that inspired this book in the first place, an event that showed me how the clinical situation can be used to understand the psychodynamics that are also occurring outside it. Hence, Chapter One will be the most highly theoretical chapter, setting out the major concepts from a relational psychodynamic perspective that will be applied throughout this book. These foundational concepts will be built upon throughout the text.

With the theoretical basis in place, Chapter Two will offer the first application of theory by way of a clinical event from my own practice that was provoked by a Google search. Chapter Three will explore what I call "the matrix", that is, the ubiquity of social technologies in our everyday life. Chapter Four will examine the dangers in which objectification plays a central role in online relating, while Chapter Five will contrarily discuss how "being in the mind of the other" is an essential aspect of intersubjective online relating. Chapter Six will consider the broader questions of how the nature of the online world can affect the experience of identity. This will be followed by some conclusions, reflections, and suggestions for future research.

I wish to close this introduction with an acknowledgement that this is not a text that aims, at the end, to proclaim today's technology as a great good or a great evil. In fact, I very much seek to avoid this kind of dichotomous judgement as much as I can. Coming across the research and social commentary, one constantly runs into what can broadly be called optimistic (and even utopian) perspectives and pessimistic (or dystopian) ways of looking at the continued development of the influence of Internet technology on our society. Naughton (2012a) notes,

> The problem with the optimist–pessimist dichotomy is that the optimists rarely address the reality of destruction [of the old ways] while the pessimists rarely acknowledge the creative possibilities of the new. We need to transcend this shouting match. (p. 182)

Another word for Naughton's "shouting match" would be dialectic: a concept with which psychoanalysis is quite familiar. It is the difficult but necessary job of the psychoanalyst to hold the dialectic, and this is what I shall seek to do throughout. Lanier (2011), in his book *You are not a Gadget*, alerts the reader early on that he is writing this book for humans, not computers. He wishes to make it abundantly clear that his book "is not antitechnology in any sense. It is pro-human" (p. ix). To this I say, "Hear! hear!"

CHAPTER ONE

Psychodynamics

"No man, for any considerable period, can wear one face to himself and another to the multitude, without finally getting bewildered as to which may be the true"

(Hawthorne, 1850)

This chapter will set out the main underlying psychodynamic principles that I propose are operating within the intersubjective system of online relating. I open the chapter by discussing how psychodynamic concepts may be deployed outside the clinic to gain insight into unconscious relational processes, before going into the main psychodynamic paradigm of relational psychoanalysis. This will be the most theoretically dense chapter of the entire book, as it lays out the conceptual basis for further developments of theory and the applications to social networking that will follow. The main aim of the chapter is to provide an overarching lens through which one can apprehend online interpersonal interaction from a relational psychodynamic perspective.

Psychodynamic applications outside the clinic

Psychoanalysis developed from within the clinical situation. It was Freud's observations with individual patients that provided the initial scaffold for the theory of psychoanalysis that was revised and worked over again and again in the light of new experiences and new evidence. No doubt theoretical dogmatism often obscured new possibilities and prevented fresh thought, ultimately creating a constellation of schools of psychoanalysis rather than a single theory undergoing successive revisions. However, the *ideal* of learning from clinical experience remained. Historically, applying the scientific method to psychoanalysis has been problematic, notably because the object of enquiry, the unconscious, is elusive to empirical observation. This, however, does not release psychoanalysis from the duty to offer evidence of its efficacy as both a treatment and a theory. Dreher (2000) addresses the problematic nature of putting the same nomothetic and quantitative tools so popular in social and empirical methods to use in psychoanalytic research. Dreher suggests an alternative to conventional research methods for psychoanalysis in which a conceptual approach may be preferred. That is:

> a class of research activities, the focus of which lies in the systematic clarification of psychoanalytic concepts . . . such research is both about the history of concepts, so as to trace a concept's origin and development, and equally about the current use of a concept, its clarification, and its differentiation. (Dreher, 2000, pp. 3–4)

She then notes that conceptual psychoanalytic research such as this is a *constructive as well as a critical tool.*

Psychoanalysis has a long history as a constructive and critical tool, not only in the clinical situation, but also as a cultural application, beginning with Freud's (admittedly often problematic) readings of cultural influences, including literature (Freud, 1907a), art (Freud, 1910c, 1914b), and religion (Freud, 1939a).

Nowadays, psychoanalytic conceptual research is being applied more and more in the development of qualitative research methodologies (Frosh, 2010; Hollway & Jefferson, 2010) in sociology, anthropology, and other social research applications. Frosh (2010), in particular, is interested in how a discipline such as psychoanalysis, which emerged from the very particular nature of the clinical encounter, *can* be utilised outside that rarefied space that is the psychoanalyst's consulting room. Frosh poignantly wonders what happens when psychoanalysis is taken out of the clinic and asks whether it would still be considered "psychoanalysis". For extra-clinical material, Frosh maintains, with some reservations, that psychoanalysis

> offers a distinctive and productive approach to interpreting human actions, social phenomena and cultural products 'outside' the clinic. If the theoretical constructs generated inside the clinic by psychoanalysis have any robustness, why should they not be at least suggestive aids to comprehension of complex events that in their unexpectedness or emotional intensity seem to show the traces of the unconscious? (Frosh, 2010, p. 4)

With respect to the psychodynamics of social networking, we will indeed be utilising psychoanalytic theory to aid us in the "comprehension of complex events" that seem to be occurring at the nexus between the medium of social networking (that is the SNSs themselves) and what might be unconsciously motivating those of us who use them.

The aim, then, is to read the phenomenon of social networking psychoanalytically, outside the clinical context, and within the larger socio-cultural sphere. This approach examines social networks themselves, inclusive of their cultural epiphenomena: the profusion of "talk" in the media about social media, which is itself distributed and promulgated over social networks. Previous psychological and quantitative research in the field of social networking will naturally be incorporated, making this work, in a sense, a meta-analysis. However, rather than seeking to create a conventional quantitative meta-analysis, described as "a statistical procedure which brings together findings from similar studies to estimate overall effects" (Cooper, 2008, p. 22), this approach will utilise existing studies by focusing a psychoanalytic lens upon them in order to interpretatively deduce psychoanalytically relational themes that may be present, both explicitly and implicitly embedded in the research.

As outlined in the introduction, this is not meant to be a comprehensive piece of research in its own right (I have carried out no new empirical research in the preparation for this book) but, rather, an interpretation of the existing research, cultural artefacts, and an ethnographically influenced reading of the state of social media and the self.

In relation to the research applications of psychoanalysis as delineated by Hollway and Jefferson (2010), researcher subjectivity is a crucial tool in bringing understanding to material in which observation among human subjects plays a major role. The psychoanalytic encounter has long taken the effect of countertransference, that is, the feelings that an analyst has in relation to their patient, as an important source of information about the patient's internal world as picked up within the unconscious person-to-person communication between analyst and patient (Heimann, 1950; Maroda, 2004). Countertransference, in particular, is noted as one of the ways in which "the psychoanalytic principle of unconscious intersubjectivity [can be used] to theorise the effect of research relationship(s) on the production and analysis of data" (Hollway & Jefferson, 2010, p. 151). Countertransference from the clinic to application outside the clinic is, however, not simply a transferable skill. Frosh (2010), for instance, is cautious about how its clinical use can be applied outside the clinical setting:

> the practice Hollway and Jefferson describe is in some important respects significantly different from the kind of exploration of unconscious material characteristic of psychoanalytic reflection on the countertransference in the clinical situation. What the researchers do is notice how a participant made them feel ... without the necessary limitations of the analytic session and contract which would allow one to understand the validity of this response. (p. 214)

Psychodynamic therapists are trained over several years to work with countertransference and have had the opportunity to work through their own unconscious material through a long commitment to their own psychotherapy, which is something few, if any, qualitative researchers will be required to do; even so, working through what material is transference, countertransference, or to what degree they are co-created is a notoriously difficult task, even for the experienced clinician. Despite all these caveats, however, I would stress that the dynamics that are occurring are identical in all human-to-human interactional settings; it is the nature of how they are provoked and worked with that limits the important differences: both contexts are mutually co-constructive in nature. I agree with Frosh's concern about the direct application of a psychoanalytic process to other kinds of research. However, I also agree with Hollway and Jefferson that thoughtful subjectivity can be utilised in ways that enhance meaning, or, at the very least, reveal researcher bias. Although I will not be taking a countertransference approach to my analysis here, I will be using psychoanalytic language to try to understand the online interaction and relational dynamics I believe to be occurring there. Mostly, however, I will be applying a version of the conceptual approach described by Dreher (2000), above. Notably, as mentioned in the introduction, I have found it important to immerse myself in SNS use throughout this process as a way to have a fully subjective experience of that which I am analysing here.

This is undoubtedly an unconventional methodology, and, by utilising it, I accept that I may be opening myself up to criticisms of being overly speculative in my approach. If this is the charge, then I accept it. Large-scale quantitative studies, as useful as they are, do not offer us much insight into the idiographic nature of an individual's psychological motivations, meaning-making, and phenomenologically subjective experiences. They do, however, offer tantalising clues as to what might be going on for individuals and in between individuals on a personal and interpersonal level. A critical psychoanalytic approach to this existing research offers a degree of flexibility and freedom to open up new ways of working through this complex material, providing a kind of insight that is not available by other means. It is here that a psychoanalytic methodology offers something new and exciting because it contains within it an interpretative approach that aims to access not just what can be witnessed and collected with *hard* quantitative data, but also allows access to the dynamics that operate under the level of consciousness. While any reader or fellow researcher ought to be wary of unbridled supposition, a degree of speculative freedom (particularly with reference to the unconscious) is necessary to free a flexible and creative approach required to address this issue from a psychoanalytic point of view. Freud (1900a), in his pioneering work *The Interpretation of Dreams*, notes that "[we psychoanalysts] are justified . . . in giving free reign to our speculations so long as we retain the coolness of our judgement and do not mistake the scaffolding for the building" (p. 536). Freud, no doubt, can be criticised for having, on several occasions, mistaken the scaffolding for the building; however, he unmistakably cracked open a new way of thinking about the human psyche in ways that continue to resonate to this day. My aim throughout this work is to demonstrate as much as possible the theoretical connections I will be making in an endeavour to maintain transparency and clarity; while I aim to be describing the building, I hope to provide enough evidence to allow the reader the opportunity to judge for themselves when the scaffolding is obscuring the edifice itself. It is my hope to provide a psychoanalytic framework in which to approach online social networks that further research may need to amend, adapt, criticise, and refine for further study in the future. Furthermore, it is my hope that this book will encourage more qualitative research into this interesting area. Throughout this text, theory will be illustrated time and again with existing material to ground the theoretical thinking within the data; to put it in the vernacular of a poker player, I hope to show my hand at all times.

Context

While the phenomenon of social networking is of great interest to a variety of psychological and sociological researchers, it is most heavily researched by those with a commercial interest in the domains of brand development and marketing research. The vast majority of the material I encountered in my research for this book made little reference to psychodynamics outside of the odd journal article or book chapter and the significant exception of Turkle's (2011) work, which has been highly influential, and a special edition of the *Psychoanalytic Review* published in 2007—by social media standards, already far out of date. Malater (2007a), in his introduction to the special issue of the *Psychoanalytic Review* lays out the challenges that the Internet offers to psychoanalysis:

> we find very different ideas on the extent to which cyberculture should be seen as posing basic challenges to current psychoanalytic thought and practice. Some authors ask what psychoanalysis can make of the Internet, while others ask what the Internet has made and will continue to make of psychoanalysis. (p. 4)

This notion that psychoanalysis needs to respond to, and be responsive towards, developments in technology is an important one, but this is a challenge that psychoanalysis as a whole has been reluctant to take up. This text will be more concerned with what psychoanalysis can offer to the understanding of online social networking than the other way round. Mental health professionals, and particularly the talking therapies, must also develop strategies with regard to both theory and practice to meet the particular challenges their clients are facing in relation to the online world.

In the context of the overwhelming presence that SNSs have in the life of contemporary individuals, it is hardly surprising that the majority of resources going into social networking research comes from the commercial sector, a sector that is naturally interested in utilising the enormous amount of data currently available for the purposes of maximising profit. This undoubtedly raises many questions about the potential for the exploitation of people as consuming objects, with commensurate concerns for privacy and social control.[5] As if these concerns were not important enough to consider with regard to relatively market-savvy adults, there is further concern for children and young people. Fortunately, not all of the research interest in children's SNS use is limited to seeing them as current and future consumers. Psychologists and sociologists are drawn to studying children to see what kind of differences may be observable in the these young people, referred to as "Digital Natives" by Palfrey and Gasser (2008), who have grown up saturated within an environment of online social networking. Technological divides that cross generational thresholds have always provoked concerns in the older generation, and online social networking is no different. It is through research, however, and not knee-jerk emotional reactions to what we do not understand, that will lead us towards a clearer understanding of what is actually going on. For younger people, current research appears to be mixed in its conclusions about the health- or pathology-giving qualities of SNSs. This is probably due to the complexity of online social networking and the difficulty of designing research to accurately reflect what is going on. Furthermore, due to its complexity, it is fair to assume at this stage that different sorts of engagements with different aspects of SNSs will dictate to a large degree how healthy or unhealthy the engagement is, making overall statements about the value of online relating unhelpful. Clarke's (2009) work demonstrates the ways in which technology has the capacity to enhance creativity and identity development in young people:

> Emerging identity is an important aspect of early adolescent development, and in our existing digital culture children have an immense

opportunity to explore their world, be creative, play with identity and experiment with different social mores. Using SNSs is not only entertaining for children, but also highly creative and allows them to assert their identity in a totally unique way, checking out what their friends think of their creative endeavours. (p. 74)

Clarke's research has demonstrated many of the positive qualities that SNSs have for young people, a finding that runs contrary to the fearful beliefs that many born after the digital revolution, those whom Palfrey and Gasser (2008) term "Digital Immigrants", hold about the Internet use of the generations below them. Contrarily, Seligman (2009) notes that although there is much more research to be done with regard to the relationship between online social connection and physical health (morbidity and mortality), he, none the less, categorises our growing reliance on virtual socialising as a growing public health problem, particularly for young people. Summarising the work of Kraut et al. (1998) on the effect of Internet use in families, Seligman states that:

greater use of the internet was associated with declines in communication between family members in the house, declines in the size of their social circle, and increases in their levels of depression and loneliness . . . Children are now experiencing less social interaction and have fewer social connections during key stages of their physiological, emotional and social development. (p. 19)

It is important to note the date of this study, which was carried about before Web 2.0 really came into force, meaning that the nature of the ease of relationality within the Internet had not yet developed to what it is today. On the other hand, the recent proliferation of tablets and smartphones (which will be addressed in Chapter Three) that have emerged since this research has taken place is likely to negatively affect family life, if only through the sheer constant distraction (and here I am referring to parents even more so than their children) they offer, which can get in the way of face-to-face relating. With the phenomenon of social networking technologies being at the same time so vast, so new, and so rapidly changing, competing conclusions about its health or pathology (mental, emotional, and physical) continues to be contradictory and research into it fraught with difficulty.

Taking a process-orientated approach offers us a fresh point of view and provides an alternative perspective in the examination of unconscious human motivation and online social networking. Psychotherapists have long known that, with the exception of behaviours that are a danger to the self and/or others, behaviour alone is not necessarily indicative of health or pathology: it is how that behaviour manifests itself within the overall experience and meaning-making of that individual. A helpful metaphor to enable us to understand the relation between behaviour and the online social network would be to think about behaviour and its relation to food. Food is necessary for life, while, at the same time, it is imbued with individual and cultural meaning. Food surrounds us and it is fundamentally plugged into everyday human experience and motivation: from sating our basic biological needs to offering itself up as a symbol of our connection to the earth, each other, and, for some, spirituality. Given its ubiquity and necessity, one could not say that *eating* is itself a healthy or pathological behaviour; it is the manner, purpose, and meaning of the eating that becomes the locus of interest into its health or pathology (Orbach, 2002, 2006). There is a wide range of behaviours in what could be construed as "healthy" eating or "unhealthy" eating. While some behaviours, such as bingeing/purging and starving oneself are clearly indicative of mental and emotional suffering,[6] the myriad relationships one might have with food require both a phenomenological report from the eater, along with some degree of interpretation to understand its underlying meaning. Orbach (2006), for example, advocates developing a fully emotional and bodily knowledge of an individual's relationship with food so one can make profound, honest, and integrated decisions about what one's needs are in relation to the consumption of his or her food towards a state of "intuitive eating"; an analogous method could be applied with regard to online engagement. Thinking in this way releases us from a dialectical good/bad relationship (in which impossible "diets" are taken on) and impels a more profound engagement composed of thoughtfully received signals from the mind and body. For example, while most fast food constitutes "bad nutrition", we would not condemn an individual who sometimes enjoys it as displaying a sign of poor mental health. Its lack of nutrition does not make fast food inherently bad, although as a society we must manage the consequences of its ease, inexpensiveness, and ubiquity (Lustig, 2012). The way in which online social networking is consumed can be based on similar principles. If we understand that interpersonal relating itself is a form of "food" in the sense of how nourishing it might be, then we can try to comprehend, phenomenologically, how its users consume it before coming to snap judgements about its health or pathology. Online social networking is often charged as being the "fast food" of interpersonal relating, and there is little doubt that it shares many of these qualities and is often used as such. However, to simply conclude that online relating is fast food, and therefore unhealthy, is to conclude without proper evaluation. Interpersonal relating is, for psychoanalysis, a crucial locus of psychological and emotional health and well being; relational templates from infanthood and youth are played out in adult attachment in gripping patterns that can last for a lifetime. Relational pathology existed long before social networks, but as social networking is becoming the site of so much interpersonal relating, it has become a new locus of interest for psychoanalysis.

Object relations

While the central theoretical axis of this text is relational, it is important to say something about the psychoanalytic school of object relations, which, as briefly outlined in the introduction, preceded relational theory and continues to take an important role in the relational perspective of the psyche. Put very briefly,[7] object relations theory moved away from Freud's drive theory (or libido theory), which was primarily interested in the individual as a repository of strong inherent drives (instincts) that sought release; the "object" was the thing that could provide the satisfaction of that drive (or need). The object, however, could be infinitely variable:

> it may be an external object, someone in the person's immediate circle for example, or part of the subject's own body. In general, the object is incidental – it is not specific to any given instance and can easily be replaced. (Quinodoz, 2004, p. 137)

While the term "object" later came primarily to represent people or parts of people, the terminology itself comes from this period in Freud's theorising, epitomised in his essay "Instincts and their vicissitudes" (1915c). Melanie Klein, a psychoanalyst seen to sit between classical Freudian theory and the development of the object relations school (Hinshelwood, 1991), shifted focus towards how these objects in the external world, to which the subject is so drawn, become important parts of the internal world as "internal objects" through the process of introjection. These theories were further developed by British psychoanalysts Fairbairn, Winnicott, and Bion, who, though going in rather different directions with the theories of the object, are generally grouped together under the broad title of the British School of Object Relations.

These theorists, in their own idiosyncratic ways, describe a system in which the process of introjection brings objects from the external world into the rich phantasy world of the unconscious of the subject. These internal objects then form relationships with each other and the ego itself *within the individual* (hence the phrase "object relations") in which

> The experience of the internal object is deeply dependent on the experience of the external object – and internal objects are, as it were, mirrors of reality. But they also contribute significantly, through projection, to the way the external objects are themselves perceived and experienced. (Hinshelwood, 1991, p. 68)

In this context, the nature of the internal objects as they influence the external world becomes the focus of analytic investigation. These internal objects affect the transference to others, that is, the internal objects as experienced by the subject may be projected on to others so that the other is perceived by the subject in the same way as an earlier relationship (e.g., an individual might see their boss as their persecuting father or abandoning mother). Taking this context as axiomatic, object relations therapy works by seeking to understand

> the role that internal object relations play in the creation and maintenance of those [external] relationships . . . The therapist–client relationship consequently would be viewed as an in-vivo expression of what is pathological about the patient's life. (Cashdan, 1988, p. 28)

In other words, the object relations therapist seeks to understand how the internal *relational world* comes to affect the external relational world of the patient: how the patient perceives others through the relational matrix of their own unconscious mind. The analyst can do this by analysing the transference, that is, by understanding how the patient responds to the analyst herself she can get some idea of what may be happening in the unconscious object relational world. As we will see, the relational perspective takes this one step further by asking how the *analyst's subjectivity* is contributing to the relational structure as well. However, the purely intrapsychic world of the subject remains an important part of the puzzle. Particularly, when we are discussing an individual's relationship to their online world, internal object relations will be at play, arguably more so than they are in face-to-face relating, because there is less relational feedback. As Lingiardi (2011) has pointed out, online life may be a very particular activity that allows for exploration of these processes:

> Online life can facilitate nonlinear experiences capable of generating states of the mind and self organizations distinct from those we experience in our off-line life. Computer-mediated communication can facilitate the exploration of aspects of our psychic functioning that, without this facilitation, could remain inaccessible or encapsulated in social prescriptions . . . Although some may well get lost in Reality 2.0, others can navigate in areas of self that they would never have allowed themselves to explore otherwise. (p. 493)

A psychodynamic approach can, no doubt, be utilised to enable closer understanding of this psychic functioning. The relational approach enables both the intrapsychic (what is going on inside one psyche) and the intersubjective (what is going on between psyches) perspectives to be acknowledged at once.

Relational psychoanalysis

In addition to being an heir to the object relations tradition, relational psychoanalysis further developed out of influences from outside the field, including disciplines such as critical theory and postmodern discourses that challenge psychoanalytic authority and epistemology, thereby deconstructing the assumed power of the psychoanalyst within the clinical setting. The process of the mutualisation of power dynamics within the clinical setting began to question how much the psychoanalyst's own object relations were present in the consulting

room and affecting the therapy, producing what came to be understood as a co-created and intersubjective therapeutic space. Although
relational psychoanalysis shares a set of common perspectives around
the issue of intersubjectivity, it is neither a unified theory nor a new
school of psychoanalysis: "[i]t lies on a level of abstraction different
from any theory, it is, rather, a metatheory, a framework or schema
that proves the necessary structure with which to go on building
coherent and comprehensive . . . theories" (Aron & Harris, 2005,
p. xviii). The diversity of the relational community offers a great deal
to the theorist hoping to apply psychoanalytic thinking to extra-clinical cultural artefacts because it is, by its nature, inter-disciplinary and
makes itself available to such applications. With its theoretical roots
firmly in object relations (alongside influences from self psychology,
interpersonal psychoanalysis, continental philosophy, feminism, and
identity politics) the relational perspective is fundamentally organised
around the principle of intersubjectivity. Aron (1996) describes this as
a shift from a "one person psychology" paradigm where, in the clinical situation, the patient is the only psychology (or psyche) in the
room (to whom the analyst becomes the neutral object) to a "two person psychology" paradigm in which both analyst and patient are seen
as two fully vital subjects with their own psychologies which interact
in the relational matrix, forever co-constructing each other. Hence,
transference, classically seen as the projection of previous relationships on to the object of the neutral analyst is, from the relational
perspective, seen as mutually co-created in the analytic encounter in
response to the analyst as subject: the analyst is fully implicated
within it. The distinction between one- and two-person psychologies
can also be termed as that which lies between the intrapsychic and
intersubjective domains. Benjamin (1988) contrasts the intrapsychic as
that "which conceives of the person as a discrete unit with a complex
internal structure" to the intersubjective which "describes capacities
that emerge in the interaction between self and others" (p. 20). While
the intersubjective view is inclusive of the intrapsychic domains of its
individuals, it maintains that

> the individual grows in and through the relationship to other subjects.
> Most important, this perspective observes that the other whom the self
> meets is also a self, a subject in his or her own right. It assumes that
> we are able and need to recognize that other subject as different and

yet alike, as an other who is capable of sharing similar mental experience. Thus the idea of intersubjectivity reorients the conception of the psychic world from a subject's relations to its object toward a subject meeting another subject. (Benjamin, 1988, pp. 19–20)

In other words, the crux of relational theory is *the nature of what happens between subjects*; a perspective that is absolutely crucial to online social networking because it is mediating so much subject-to-subject relating. This intersubjective point of view runs in contrast to classical psychoanalytic theory that was primarily interested in intrapsychic phenomena, both from a developmental perspective (how an infant developed as a subject in relation to "the mother", usually conceptualised as an object) and clinically (how the patient-as-subject orientates herself to the analyst as object[8]). The model of the intrapsychic and intersubjective is useful in understanding how an individual might interact with an online social network, an interaction (like any other) that necessarily involves and provokes both of these operations. From this perspective, the subject is no longer perceived as being located within a completely cohesive being in isolation; rather, he exists both internally (intrapsychically) and between himself and another; in many ways, he can only experience himself as existing in this in-between space. In other words, "*Mind has been redefined from a set of predetermined structures emerging from inside an individual organism to transactional patterns and internal structures derived from an interactive interpersonal field*" (Mitchell, 1988, p. 17, original italics). In our online world, in which an individual is alone interfacing with a computer screen, though in constant interaction with others that are "out there" also interacting alone with computer screens, this approach seems right on the money.

The true self, the false self, and the persona[9]

In the relational paradigm, we conceive of the intrapsychic apparatus as always operating within the larger relational matrix: what also might be called intersubjective space. The British psychoanalyst Winnicott occupies a historically influential place in the development of relational theory, though relational theory as a discipline and appellation only developed after his death in 1971. His work in the British

object relations tradition has come to be seen, with hindsight, as fundamentally relational in nature. Winnicott's (1964) axiom that "there is no
such thing as an infant" is designed to indicate that the infant does not
exist outside its relationship with its mother.[10] For Winnicott, the
psychological success of this infant is dependent upon good-enough
mothering and an appropriate facilitating environment.[11] One of the
most important components of the facilitating environment is what
Winnicott (1960) refers to as "holding", which will be crucial in the
development of the infant's subjectivity. Holding represents both the
literal physical holding of the infant alongside the psychological and
emotional holding by the primary care-taker, but, more specifically, ".
. . it refers to a three-dimensional or space relationship with time gradually added" (Winnicott, 1960, p. 589). The holding phase allows for
the ego to integrate and differentiate others from the self; it is the
beginning of a cohesive selfhood and intelligence, and "the beginning
of a mind as something distinct from the psyche . . . symbolic functioning, and of the organization of a personal psychic content
[personal narrative], which forms a basis for dreaming and for living
relationships" (p. 590). This shift during the holding phase is closely
bound up with the infant's change from being merged with the mother
to being separate from her, or to relating to her as separate and "not-
me"; the infant begins to experience integration, but also regresses
back to disintegration during moments of stress.

As we progress, we can see how this holding environment is
replicated in online relating in a way that can also provoke feelings of
integration and disintegration, dependent on feelings of being recognised or misrecognised or, as we shall see, in relation to presentations
of the false or true self across the network. Winnicott's deeply intersubjective approach can be contrasted to Freud's perspectives on
psychic development, which are much more focused on the infant's
internal world, largely excluding the real others that will have influenced that infant/adult. From this tradition, the earliest intrapsychic
models of the personality continue to be Freud's tripartite model of
the id, ego, and superego. This model still remains a useful shorthand
in referring to the passions/instincts (id), the agency that operates
between the internal and external worlds (ego), and that which
observes and judges these interactions (superego).

Winnicott's (1956) development of the false self and Jung's
(1966) alternative but related concept of the persona are models of

intrapsychic operation that broadly rest upon Freud's original model of the tripartite psyche. Although they are from divergent schools of psychoanalysis, they have a lot in common. Both persona and false self can be described as ego functions, as they both lie between internal experience (intrapsychic) and the outside world (intersubjective); hence, they can both be conceived as "relational" because they develop for the purpose of managing the space between self and other. Samuels (2013) notes that Jung's work on alchemy reflects a Jungian position that is profoundly relational in nature, "it is like a chemical combination . . . two or more substances are mixed and their natures are transformed and a new *third thing* is created". Samuels relates this "third thing" to Ogden's (1999) psychoanalytic "third", which will be discussed in Chapter Two. Both the false self and persona function in an outside-facing way by utilising the reality principle to prevent id-orientated aims[12] from expressing themselves in ways which are socially unacceptable. To this end, they both require that one interacts with the world in a partial way, leaving aspects of one's subjectivity more or less unexpressed and unrecognised by the other. For Jung (1966), "[t]he persona is a complicated system of relations between individual consciousness and society . . . a kind of mask, designed on the one hand to make a definite impression upon others, and, on the other, to conceal the true nature of the individual" (p. 192). The persona, for Jung, is not essentially pathological because it develops as a natural mediator between the internal and external world. Pathology develops only when the individual identifies with their persona at the expense of the other attributes of their personality: when they believe the persona to be "the whole thing". These ideas of partiality in the presentation of self with regard to online life should be self-evident, and will be applied throughout this text in more detail.

Although Winnicott's false self developed independently out of the emerging school of object relations, as opposed to the school of analytical psychology founded by Jung, it does have resonances with Jung's model of the persona. Like the persona, Winnicott's concept of the false self is also a result of natural developmental processes. Although it arises as a defence of the true self, this defence (as in Jung's conceptualisation) is not necessarily pathological unless the false self obliterates an internal relation to the true self. For Winnicott (1956)

This false self is no doubt an aspect of the true self. It hides and protects it, and it reacts to the adaptation failures and develops a pattern corresponding to the pattern of environmental failure. In this way the true self is not involved in reacting, and so preserves a continuity of being. (p. 387)

The defensive structure lies in the way in which the false self preserves a continuity of being: a continuity that is threatened by impingement, virtual or otherwise. Interestingly, for Winnicott, the false self is *an aspect of the true self*; this is an internal relation that is crucial to retain in relation to our application of these concepts to how an individual negotiates her online social world. Unfortunately, the use of the word "false" frequently gives the reductive impression of a self that is sort of a fake "add-on" that would be better off dispensed with. Alternatively, the false self should be seen as a deployment of the ego that is a creative response to a deficit: the false self arises specifically to meet this challenge. The false self is the outward aspect of the psyche that takes on the role of a great deal of interpersonal work, work such as being nice, saying the right thing, getting on with people, and *doing what is expected*. In these circumstances, the false self is taking on the job of the social role so that the true self can carry on being. This is similar to the "masking" role that Jung (1966), gives to the persona in order to face outwardly towards society. Although it is a mask, it is a particular sort of mask that is suited to the individual in some way, even if it distorts access to the real self, so to call it "false" is not completely accurate: to call it partial would be more so.

While this is a system that is brilliantly conceived to manage both internal and external worlds, there is, no doubt, a rub. The rub is that while the psyche as a whole seeks recognition, it is those agencies of the ego that lean heavily on false self and persona that tend to receive this recognition simply because, by their very nature, these functions are outward facing; the nature of outward-facing SNSs naturally invites presentations from the false self. The result of this can leave the true, or real, self feeling invisible and unrecognised, and, at the deepest level, unloved. To use a metaphor, it is as if, in the theatre of life, there are a whole series of actors milling about the stage, but the spotlight lands on only one or two; while they bask in the glow, the others (equally representative of aspects of the self) are left invisible to the outside world, and begin to feel like invisible understudies. While these actors are necessary, the rub "rubs" when the false self offers a compliance towards the demands of the social world that can become split off: the compliant self operating for social sanction and positive social feedback gets taken for the whole thing, rather than an aspect of the person. Winnicott (1982a) draws a similar metaphor regarding actors themselves:

> there are those who can be themselves and who also can act, whereas there are others who can only act, and who are completely at a loss when not in a role, and when not being appreciated or applauded (acknowledged as existing). (p. 150)

Should an individual have a proclivity (through early parenting) towards acting all the time, Winnicott (1982a) warns that "compliance is then the main feature, with imitation as a specialty" (p. 147) which is no doubt related to narcissism, as will be discussed further in Chapter Four. Both Jung and Winnicott, in their idiosyncratic ways, draw attention to the nature of these *partial* aspects of the psyche that have a necessary role in the public-facing side of our subjectivity while carrying with them the continued risk that their partial role may be misrecognised by both the individual and those around her as the full representation of the self.

SNSs such as Facebook and Twitter, as outward-facing technologies, particularly call upon the persona and the false self accordingly. They are, *par excellence*, the social world manifested online and require the activation of these public-facing psychic agencies more than any other. This perspective becomes particularly clear when we see that the main role of the false self for Winnicott (1982a) is to "hide and protect the True Self" (p. 142). In extreme cases the "False Self sets up as real and it is this that observers tend to think is the real person ... at this extreme the True Self is hidden" (p. 142–143). For Jung (1966), the persona does a similar job; it is "designed on the one hand to make a definite impression upon others, and on the other, to conceal the nature of the individual" (p. 192). The potential trouble here with regard to online relating is not that we have a false self or persona, it is more that SNSs might encourage us in some ways to emphasise these aspects of our psyche at the expense of others. For Winnicott, pathology appears when a deep and dissociating split occurs between the false and real self, and for Jung (1966) it is when one identifies with his own persona to the consequence that "he no longer knows himself" (p. 192); what he knows, Jung implies, is only the partial expression of the self that is outward facing. In both instances, the dynamic between the two agencies remain in a delicate balance in relation to the outside world, liable to tip into pathology when leaning too much into false self or persona, or opening up too much vulnerability when exposing too much unprotected unconscious material to an external world that might not respond with care. SNSs can be seen as just another public space in which these same dynamics are called into action. After all, we protect the more vulnerable parts of ourselves in a variety of other real-life circumstances, why would we not do so on a very public SNS?

In many ways, it is much easier for others to express and apprehend the nature of our false selves or personae than other aspects of the psyche, for several reasons: they are the social-facing façades of our subjectivities, they are our most practised public faces, and they are the most easily observed by others. For these reasons, it tends to be the false self/persona that becomes the vehicle for our self-expression on status updates and tweets, to the exclusion of other aspects of our wide ranging and multiple subjectivities. In expressing ourselves in this fashion, we are protecting aspects of our subjectivities that we feel less happy about projecting into the world. Of course, just as in real life, different individuals are happy to expose very different sorts of things to the outside world; while for some it might be their "OKness", for others it might, in just the same way, be that they are not "OK". At the same time, the public self, as displayed across a social network, can lack the subtlety and complexity of a full subjectivity as experienced in face-to-face interactions. Winnicott (1982a) understands the true self as beginning from birth as spontaneous and unencumbered "sensori-motor aliveness" (p. 149). In other words, the unguarded and visceral spontaneity of the infant is, in essence, its true self. Once engagement with the outside world begins to impinge on this spontaneous way of being, the false self develops to protect it by taking on the role of interfacing with the external word. Deployed in this way, the false self contributes to positive psychic health, engendering rational defences to meet the impingements and deficits always present in the relational world (nobody, after all, can be ideally met). These defences, which, over time, develop into our everyday and unconscious relational dynamics, are at play in every interaction in the online social networking world; it is the very nature of our extension into virtual space, which is always cognisant of the imagined other, or what boyd (2007) calls "invisible audiences". When observers (on or offline) tend to think the false self is the whole real person, the spontaneous true self notices that it lacks the recognition that the false self commands. To follow Jung's reasoning, the dangers lie not just in others believing the false self to be the whole thing, the greater risk is that the individual himself comes to believe it as real. Hence, the question becomes, how does an individual relate to his or her own representation of him or herself on the SNS? The answer to this question, of course, lies within the individual.

Depending on the degree of splitting or lack of integration between the true and false selves, the recognition received by the false self will be felt as a *lack* of recognition to the true self. In this, the subject might feel as if the recognition were adulterated in some way, and meant for something that is "not me", that is, meant for the performing false self rather than the true self. The disturbing result is that a really effective false self, the one often found in narcissistic personalities, is quite good at attracting a certain kind of attention (altered recognition) but it derives this attention in way that the true self cannot assimilate. The common experience that many people have of feeling fraudulent and harbouring fears of being "found out" are embedded in the dynamic of this split between the true and false selves. Too much investment in the false self serves to disable the true self's ability to experience an authentic and spontaneous expression under the gaze of the other: "Only the True Self can be creative and only the True Self can feel real. Whereas a True Self feels real, the existence of a False Self results in feeling unreal or a sense of futility" (Winnicott, 1982a, p. 148). In bringing our application of these concepts to online social networking, we need to ask what it is that the SNSs ask of us. What aspect of the self is being called to account for itself? Negotiating this paradigm is fraught with complex issues, such as what is being sought through the social network and what is motivating that seeking.

While both Winnicott and Jung's models offer a useful shorthand to understanding public and private identities within the self, more contemporary models view identity with a great deal more complexity in relation to social construction, power, politics, and multiplicity. Although neither Winnicott nor Jung were simplistic in their own thinking about these concepts (both are richly and complexly drawn out by their theorists), identity theory has continued to develop in response to postmodernism, which has concerned itself with the multiple and fluid nature of identity as it is embedded in culture; this will be discussed further in relation to SNSs in Chapter Six. Throughout this text, however, we continue to use the terms false self, true self, and persona as a useful shorthand, while recognising that subjectivity and identity are far more complex than the seemingly simple terminology seems to indicate.

Recognition

The functioning of the false self/persona and the true/real self is a fundamental component in the response to the intersubjective dynamics of recognition. The seeking of recognition is foundational to relating in that it works both ways: the desire to be recognised and the desire to discover and recognise the other (Benjamin, 1988). This interplay of seeking recognition while at the same time seeking to recognise is a dialectical tension that commences from the very start of life within the infant–mother dyad, where initial relational templates are laid down through to adult life, where they are repeated, worked through, and, ideally, amended, repaired, and developed further towards the capacity for intimacy. Benjamin (1988), who pioneered thinking on recognition and its role in relational processes, notes that an individual caught in a false self identification may

> feel unreal to himself, with the deadness and despair that accompany the sense of unreality . . . one of the most important elements in feeling authentic . . . [is] the recognition of an outside reality that is not one's own projection, the experience of contacting other minds. (p. 37)

Part of the thrill of online social networking is the experience of engaging with other minds, despite the fact that this engagement is so frequently made remotely, when one is alone. The relation between postings on any online social network can be broadly aligned with Gabbard's (2001) thinking about the paradox of the email,

> The person sending an email message is alone, but not alone. The apparent privacy allows for freer expression, but the awareness of the

other receiving the email allows for passionate attachment and highly emotional expressiveness. The Internet has led to new definitions of privacy as well as of intimacy. (p. 734)

Interpersonal communications online (email or through SNSs) are quite limited in contrast to the myriad of relational cues that provide so much information in real life (facial expressions, tone of voice, body language, etc.) and the environment is open for projection: a dynamic that gets in the way of authentic relating and mutual recognition. While the dialectic between false–true self and personal–real self offers us a toehold into the intrapsychic nature of engagement, recognition gives us the key to relational processes.

While intersubjectivity is the *sine qua non* of relational thinking, recognition is the deceptively simple concept that acts as the philosopher's stone that lies at the very centre of it. Recognition is fundamentally relational in the sense that it absolutely depends upon the gaze of an "other", an event that is experienced as both intrapsychic and intersubjective. Benjamin (1988), states that

> Recognition is so central to human existence as to often escape notice . . . it appears to us in so many guises that it is seldom grasped as an overarching concept . . . to recognize is to affirm, validate, acknowledge, know, accept, understand, empathize, take in, tolerate, appreciate, see, identify with, find familiar . . . love. (pp. 15–16)

Consider all the verbs in the extract above and one can begin to sense the relevance of recognition in the social networking paradigm: each of them can be seen to be mediated, activated, sought, denied, and returned across SNSs. The simple use of the "like" button on Facebook can be utilised with one simple click to affirm, validate, acknowledge, accept, appreciate, and find familiar. It is the simplicity of the click that offers, with frightening ease, access to experiences of recognition while, at the same time, risking narrowing the emotional bandwidth of the very materiality of recognition. Like it or not, recognition is being traded like a commodity across social networks; it is, indeed, the fuel that is driving users to them in droves. Recall Turkle's (2011) above-mentioned pithy statement: "technology proposes itself as the architect of our intimacies" (p. 1). This statement, in a mere nine wisely chosen words, describes precisely the way in which online social networking technology proposes itself, by way of recognition, as the architect of these intimacies as they are mediated online. While the user engagement of an SNS is often imagined to be solitary, it is clear that the drive for recognition from another is built into the very intention of these networks. Andrew Bosworth, Facebook's director of engineering, demonstrates this in a statement he made when he was describing the interactive nature of Facebook in comparison to the hardware devices made by Apple, "Your Apple product might actually still be fun without your friends. Facebook is just the most boring product on the Internet without your friends" (Greene, 2012, p. 74). It is this very interaction that Benjamin (1988) describes as being something that is sought for the self, while at the same time it is being sought with regard to the other: it is mutual,

> the necessity of recognizing as well as being recognized by the other . . . the idea of mutual recognition is crucial to the intersubjective view; it implies that we actually have a need to recognize the other as a separate person who is like us yet distinct. (p. 23)

The capacity to develop mutual recognition, as described here, is derived from the model of the mother–infant relationship in which "[t]he subject gradually becomes able to recognise the other person's subjectivity, developing the capacity for attunement and tolerance of difference" (Benjamin, 1990, p. 33). This is a developmental advance in which the infant begins to see its primary care-taker as a subject rather than an object.[13] It is a relation that ideally requires "emotional attunement, mutual influence, affective mutuality, [and] sharing states of mind" (p. 16). Mutuality is also reflected within the social network, though, as we will see, its architecture leaves it open to some perversions of both the aim to be recognised and the ways in which recognition from others may or may not hit its mark. For Benjamin, *"Recognition is the essential response, the constant companion of assertion. The subject declares, 'I am, I do,' and then waits for the response, 'You are, you have done"* (p. 21, my italics). As we saw in the previous section, this "I" will have various components of true and false self and persona. In the interpersonal space, both subjects are interacting from one complex true–false self subject to another. Across two of the major social networking platforms, Facebook and Twitter, this underlying dynamic of "I am" seeking a "you are" in response is wired into their architecture via the Facebook actions of "liking", "poking", and commenting on status updates, and via Twitter by way of following, "favoriting", "retweeting", and replying. Such interactions are offered up with great ease across a social network. Conversely, in real life, a healthy mutuality can be difficult to achieve as it depends upon a complex dialectic of oneness and separateness in the matrix of the true and false selves which offers up an axis of difference that can be challenging, particularly with regard to whatever capacities might be present due to one's experience of early relationships:

> In the ideal balance, a person is able to be fully self-absorbed or fully receptive to the other, he is able to be alone or together. In a negative cycle of recognition, a person feels aloneness is only possible by obliterating the intrusive other, that attunement is only possible by surrendering to the other. (Benjamin, 1988, p. 28)

This is a developmental achievement that is fundamentally related to true and false self; that is, recognition goes nowhere if it is the false self solely (or even mostly) that is being recognised. This is a particular danger in online social networking because of the partial revelation of self that is possible across the SNS and the ease with which a form of recognition is deployed through this architecture. Most social technology operates via quick interactions that can sometimes be at the expense of the more complex dynamics described by Benjamin.

An example of the difference between being present for real-life relational exchange and the alternative of simply being a conduit of information is exemplified by philosopher and computer scientist Jaron Lanier (2011) when he describes an experience in which he was speaking to a large audience about his book *You Are Not A Gadget*. After introducing himself, he asked audience members not to tweet or blog while he was speaking.[14] Lanier explains that he made this request

> Not out of respect for me ... but out of respect [for the audience] themselves. If something I said was memorable enough to be worthy of a tweet or a blog post later on ... then that meant what I said would have had the time to be weighed, judged, and filtered in someone's brain. Instead of [members of the audience] just being a passive relay for me ... what was tweeted, blogged, or posted on a Facebook wall would then be *you*. Giving yourself the time and space to think and feel is crucial to your existence ... *you have to find a way to be yourself before you can share yourself* (p. ix, my italics)

The danger in the social network is that it can sometimes jump the important process *of being with something*, almost always in communication with another, that is, being actively and emotionally engaged by a given internal process before passing it on, or, in Lanier's words, being more than a passive relay of information. Such is the compulsion to share and the ease with which one can do so, online social networking has the capacity to bypass the more difficult navigation of relational complexity. That is, how one navigates between being present as a full subject in relation to an other who is also a full subject, yet different. Benjamin (1988) notes that "one of the most important insights of intersubjective theory is that sameness and difference exist simultaneously in mutual recognition" (p. 47). Managing similarity is much easier than managing difference just as much in real life as it is online; online social networking in all its forms offers an architecture through which this merging of sameness and difference will be mediated: an architecture which is neither good nor bad, nor neutral.

So many concepts, so little time

Each of the general psychodynamic concepts described above are largely laid down in early life, yet continue to remain active throughout one's lifetime. Because they are instigated through primary relationships, relationships in later life continue to challenge these early templates by inviting both repetition of old styles of relating and new potentials to relate differently. Engagement across SNSs is fundamentally relational in nature and calls upon these object relational and intersubjective components that we have been discussing. The concepts I have chosen to elaborate upon in this chapter are only a small selection of possible psychodynamic applications that can be brought to bear upon online social networking. Furthermore, each concept has a long history and a complex theoretical underpinning, which is demonstrated in the many tomes dedicated to examining the nature of each of these concepts alone. The scope of this book has naturally required a reductionism in theoretical descriptions, both to accommodate a rather wide application of psychodynamics to SNSs, and also to allow a wider audience to appreciate the possibilities that a psychodynamic perspective may bring to this venture. It is my hope that others will develop the use of psychoanalytic concepts for the further study of this material. This book presumes to make a start.

CHAPTER TWO

On searching and being sought[15]

"The individual discovers himself within an interpersonal field
of the interactions in which he has participated long before the
dawn of his own self-reflective consciousness"

(Mitchell, 1993, p. 132)

These days, online social networking sites are an important locus through which the psychodynamic functions described in the previous chapter are often mediated. However, there is another domain of the Internet, though not an SNS, which, none the less, requires investigation from a psychodynamic perspective first. That is, the most omnipresent function of online life, the Google search. According to the web information company Alexa (2012), Google is the most visited website in the world, followed closely by Facebook. It is the ubiquity of Google that captures our attention here, not so much as a tool to acquire information about *things* across the Internet, but also to gain information about ourselves and people that are known to us. Vanderbilt (2013) describes how, as the Google search has developed, it has become more reflective and responsive to the multitude of search queries it receives, responds to, and learns from.

"We once used search engines to look for information," notes Vander-bilt, "now we use search to find *us* – what once seemed transactional now seems an extension of ourselves" (p. 107). Behind the scenes, search engines like Google go about the virtual business of organising "entities" into a "knowledge graph" that contains more than 500 million of these entities (Vanderbilt, 2013, p. 107); Facebook, alterna-tively, uses what it calls a "social graph". These entities become online id*entities* that are constructed around real human individuals. Such online id*entities* are compiled *on behalf of* individuals, mostly outside of their control, resulting in what I call a passive online id*entity* (as opposed to an active online identity which may be deployed via a social networking profile or personal website); it is Google that *actively* manages our online identities, while the subjects of those identities can only passively look on. There are businesses that, for a price, will offer to manage your online reputation. In reality, they only maintain the capacity to influence the organisation of content about you online, increasing the chances that the links you prefer will rise to the top of a Google search under your name; other information remains online, it just takes a bit more effort to locate it.

Knowing me, knowing you

While social networks like Facebook may be unwieldy with regard to their privacy settings, there is, none the less, more than just an illusion of control over what a person chooses to share and with whom to share it (though one can never guarantee that these rules will remain stable). It does not work this way on Google, where information about an individual from a single source can be radically disseminated quickly across the Internet and collated in a Google search for anyone to find. Today, there is nothing unusual about Googling a potential date, an employer or employee, a partner's ex-partner, or even one's potential psychotherapist. As each person has little control about what is collated, the Google search provides only a fragmented view of someone through the elements of his or her life that happen to have gone online, whether it is winning the custard contest at the village fete or having been accused of paedophilia. In this sense, online iden-tities are pre-packaged and ready for quick consumption, creating an automatic, externally "cobbled-together" identity,[16] an identity that can hang like a ghost between individuals, affecting their interpersonal relations to varying degrees. This passive cobbled-together online identity operates both intrapsychically and intersubjectively, becoming a part of how we view ourselves, our concerns about how we are viewed by others, and the way others actually view us. As we will see, it is this virtually constructed *identity* that exists like a "ghosted middle" between our embodied subjectivities and how we appear on Google that enables a variety of psychodynamic responses that contribute to the way in which recognition is deployed in the virtual world.

While the functions of online relating and identity construction will be examined more fully in Chapter Six, the context of Google, in particular, will be examined here in the face of a series of questions it provokes in relation to self-conception and concerns about how others see us:

- How does a readily available assembly of a Google id*entity*, if not *our* identity, affect the sense of our own subjectivity in relation to it?
- Is there a relational co-construction of identity between what we feel to be ourselves, what we see represented online, and the nature of other people's perspectives of us as embodied subjectivities *and* unbound virtual selves?
- How does the nature of this virtually constructed ghosted middle affect people at various stages of their relationships, from first impressions to times when such information is acquired later in the relationship?

The nature of the therapeutic encounter enables a particular kind of space to examine these questions, a space that is free of the technological distractions that are coming under scrutiny. In the consultation room, ideally at least, the old rules still apply: the patient's time will not be interrupted by ringing phones and the psychotherapist will not be multi-tasking while half-listening to the patient's material: an experience all too familiar outside this special space. Importantly, confidential material from the patient's life will not be broadcast across the Internet. If the therapeutic setting is about anything, it is about the therapist's being absolutely present for the patient, maintaining that traditional sense of "evenly suspended attention" (Freud, 1912e,

p. 111), or whatever variation the contemporary psychotherapist chooses. In this sense, the therapeutic encounter appears to be safe from the intrusions of the virtual world that are becoming so central to contemporary life. Although the hour itself is, ideally, free from these intrusions, they are, none the less, present in the minds of psychotherapists and their patients. It is not only the stories that patients bring to their sessions that involve virtual-world *content*, but *process*, too, is impinging on the precious therapeutic space. There is little doubt that patients will be Googling their potential therapists long before the first meeting and that this Googling will, in many unknown ways, affect the ways in which the therapist will be related to and seen. Hartman (2011) reminds us that it is not just patients doing the Googling, but that this curiosity has extended to affect the curiosity of therapists, too:

> Haven't we [psychotherapists] also searched the web and told ourselves there was no harm in looking? Or Googled a patient to confirm a hunch spawned by unfettered countertransference? What degree of emotional engagement in online experience then counts as 'responsible' or 'real' or 'related'. (p. 476)

Google not only offers us information about others and ourselves, however fragmented or accurate, it also offers this information with an ease of access never before available. The kind of information one can find today with a half-diligent Google search would have required the services of a private detective just some years ago. The planning, cost, and commitment of that would have deterred most (and alert them to the fact that their motivations might be transgressive); today, we simply do not encounter these obstacles or the potential consequences that come with them. With regard to the information that is found on a Google search, one can find a distinction between an intentionally packaged web presence that an individual might have created via their own personal or professional website (an active online identity), and all the other information that might be found on the Internet about them that is outside that person's control. In the particular case of the psychotherapeutic encounter, the information that patients come bearing will infiltrate the transference and affect the way in which the therapist is perceived; no doubt this works the other way around for therapists Googling their patients. The likelihood that this will be in play demands a thoughtful therapeutic response within the professional world of psychotherapy itself, and, perhaps more importantly, by acknowledging that the rarefied encounter in the consultation room, *where the unconscious relational dynamics occurring between therapist and patient are the very subject of enquiry,* can enable an understanding of these events *outside the therapeutic encounter and inside culture and society.*

What follows is an extended case vignette from my own practice. This vignette is the only "case history" from my own practice in this text, so it will be a necessary digression to make before moving back into the broader applications that this clinical experience provoked. To begin, this therapeutic event produced what I came to understand as a *virtual impingement.* A virtual impingement can be understood to be an event that happens online that impinges upon the psychological space of an individual and disrupts the capacity of that individual's "going on being" (Winnicott, 1982b). For Winnicott, an impingement occurs when the facilitating environment (and particularly the mother) fails to adapt appropriately to the infant's needs, causing "a reaction in the infant, and the reaction breaks up the going-on-being" (p. 86). A virtual impingement can be seen as analogous to this between any individual and an event that impinges on them from their virtual environment.

In this case, the virtual impingement was caused by my patient finding out information about me through a Google search that, due to his state of mind at the time, created a great deal of anxiety and anger. The first therapeutic task, of course, was to respond to its immediate effects by containing the intense feelings that were being experienced; this was followed by a more detailed therapeutic process that would allow my patient and I to extract meaning from the experience locally, that is, in relation to his (and our) psychodynamics. This local experience between my patient and me provided the original material that started me thinking about global online experience, virtual impingement, and the broader sociocultural online environment. This ultimately resulted in an exploration of relational dynamics in response to virtual impingement events that I postulate are occurring between individuals across social networks and Google searches everyday. The local clinical experience can be used to extrapolate, in the first instance, what might be going on outside the consulting room in the face of virtual impingements in general. The event I am about to convey was my first explicit experience of a virtual impingement that made itself known in my consulting room in a way that absolutely demanded my attention. One of the demands on my attention was the fact that the virtual impingement directly involved information about me. While it was my patient that initially felt the impingement so forcefully, I was impinged upon, too, by the loss of my privacy, and the way in which this loss had proved to be so hurtful to my patient. Privacy is a major concern in "reality 2.0", a term that Hartman (2011) uses to describe how Web 2.0 has affected our lives even in "the real world". In this new, virtually infused world, Hartman notes,

> Privacy is a thing of the past: just imagine who it is possible for you to be; just find what you need to know. In Reality 2.0, access trumps the need to accept limits as a tool to self-discovery. Networking replaces containment as the bulwark of meaning. (p. 473)

Important to note here is the combination of ease of access with the question of what happens to information, meaning, and containment, processes that will be discussed in the light of this vignette. It would be impossible to share this story without revealing personal information about myself, as it was this very personal information that provoked the virtual impingement. Like much material that can be found online, the information itself was rather trivial and benign, but no less out of my control and, hence, no longer private. It was the revelation of personal information outside of "containment as the bulwark of meaning" that was summoned up on a Google search that provoked the event under discussion here.

It happened in my own "private" time . . .

In order to understand the nature of the virtual impingement as a general dynamic "out in the world", I offer an illustrative case vignette in relation to an actual virtual impingement that occurred to my client Thomas[17] during his therapy with me. First, it is necessary to first digress into a seemingly unrelated event that occurred to me, alone, about eighteen months previous to the moment I learnt that Thomas has been virtually impinged upon. This is a rather bizarre story that begins one evening in 2005 when I was up late writing in my office/consultation room, which at the time was located in my home. In the quietness of the late hour, I heard a low-volume, preternatural clicking sound emanating from a pile of books and papers near the wall. I stopped working to listen more closely, at which point the disturbing clicking was followed by the sound of rustling papers. I got up from the table and approached the pile with mild trepidation, readying myself to see a mouse scamper out from under it. When this did not happen, my curiosity forced me to lift some papers and other materials off the top of the pile to locate the source of the sound. On this closer inspection, rather than revealing the rodent I had been expecting, I encountered a fiendish, prehistoric-looking, nine-inch centipede whose scorpion-like carapace glistened under the incandescent light of my office. Its multitude of razor-sharp undulating legs carried it up the wall with a surreal quality of breath-taking speed and agility. In a state of shock, I dashed off to my kitchen to find a container large enough to capture it and ultimately managed to trap it inside (the sound of the thing's legs on the thin plastic of the Tupperware doesn't bear describing).

Realising that this strange animal was not native to the UK, I arranged a meeting with the chief entomologist at the Natural History Museum early the next morning. The entomologist quickly identified that the centipede was indeed an interloper to Britain: it was classified as a *Scolopendra Gigantea*—the largest species of venomous centipede in the world. Its monstrous visual impact accurately indicated that it was indeed both poisonous and dangerous to humans, capable of injecting a necrotising poison that had the capacity to cause great pain and injury to an adult and could be fatal to a small child. Its presence in the UK was unusual, and for this reason it was of great interest to the museum. I was relieved to hand it over and obliged when the press secretary asked if she could use this story in the museum's monthly magazine; I had not anticipated that Natural History Museum would then transmit a press release later on that would make my centipede saga the most emailed story in the world the following day. The event had copious radio coverage and all the British broadsheets and tabloids covered the story; I was later able to trace the article across dozens of foreign national papers—including Taiwan's biggest daily, the *Sydney Morning Herald*, and *USA Today*, to small dailies like *The Sacramento Bee*. Each newspaper mentioned "psychotherapist, Aaron Balick" alongside information that included my age and the location of my home/office. There was a flurry of interest over the coming days, but eventually the furore died down, and the centipede story was over—at least as far as I was aware. What I was unaware of, however, was that behind the scenes each of these headlines and accompanying stories was being collected and collated by Google, creating what would become an "Aaron Balick" entity on Google's knowledge graph that would remain online for the foreseeable future: my online identity would be forever coupled with this surreal story. The amount of information about the centipede and me, for a period at least, dwarfed any other information about me on the Internet; it was, for some time, the whole of my online identity. While this kind of identity distortion is rather benign, as it indicates very little about my actual personality or my work that should concern me, none the less it occupied a massive part of my virtual self that, for a time at least, cast a disproportionate cybershadow on my online iden-*tity*. This Google representation of my online self invites a kind of *online misrecognition* where a small but interesting aspect of a life story is misrepresented through Google. There is a resonant correlation here to the idea of a false self, only in this case the false self is not a partial representation of my ego's public-facing persona, but, rather, a false public-facing Google entity constructed without my knowledge or consent. I was aware of none of these simmering psychodynamics at the time. In fact, I thought it was an amusing story and the experience provided me with a rather entertaining anecdote to tell. However, as time went on, I came to realise that online reputation was becoming a concern and such misrecognitions may have consequences. Even these concerns were nascent, mostly the centipede event was a non-story right up until it surprisingly provoked a virtual impingement that went right to the centre of an otherwise "safe" yet vulnerable therapeutic relationship.

Creating containment in therapeutic space

Although several of my patients had seen the news story when it was released, and some joked about it with me in their sessions, I had decided not to share the story with those who had not mentioned it, and for this reason had chosen not to share it with Thomas. In fact, the virtual impingement did not occur in relation to Thomas until many months after the story had completely dropped from my mind. Thomas had come to see me initially due to panic attacks and other anxiety reactions he had been experiencing because of serious allegations that were made against him in the workplace. Although Thomas was innocent of any wrongdoing, the allegations were shameful and resonated with unresolved issues of shame from his youth. Furthermore, had these allegations been made public, they would have become utterly destructive to his career prospects for the future. Because Thomas was highly invested in his career (it was practically a vocation), a threat to his professional identity was experienced as a threat to his very self. Thomas and I had been doing some very difficult therapeutic work together during this period, working to contain his anxieties and enable him to face the challenges he was encountering. Ultimately, the employer's evidence was flimsy and the allegations were neither fully pursued nor brought to light outside the workplace; however, the whole ordeal did result in Thomas having to leave his job anyway, as it was impossible for everyone that he remain in post after the acrimonious investigation. Although he was able to leave without having his reputation besmirched, his parting was difficult and followed by a serious depression which was accompanied by occasional suicidal thoughts; a long period of uncertainty and unemployment followed, through which Thomas worked courageously in his therapy. Naturally, such a life event brings up long buried feelings of early emotional trauma, which was indeed what was coming up for Thomas. During this period Thomas came to depend on me, and our relationship became a very important and sustaining one.

There are a number of ways to describe the circumstances that allow good therapeutic work to be accomplished. Most research points to the quality of the therapeutic relationship (Cooper, 2008), part of which requires what Clarkson (2003) calls the "developmentally needed or reparative relationship" to work through the developmental deficits described in Chapter One. In order for this to occur, the therapeutic alliance must provide a *"safe containing holding relationship"* (p. 148). This "holding" is resonant with Winnicott's conception, as discussed in the previous chapter, with the maternal facilitating environment. By the time the virtual impingement had occurred, Thomas and I had come close to achieving this kind of relationship, but sometimes it felt more present than others. When two people come together in the therapeutic endeavour, their intersubjectivity in the context of the therapeutic good creates something that is more than the sum of its two parts. This greater part is what Ogden (1999) calls the "analytic third", described as "a third subject, unconsciously co-created by analyst and analysand, which seems to take on a life of its own in the interpersonal field between them" (p. 487). This complex idea of the "third" is elaborated by Slochower (2005), who notes how the third is developed through a holding process that

> transforms the separate subjectivities of patient and analyst in the direction of increased synchrony. This leaves the analyst with the task of retaining, largely unexpressed, an image of the wider area created by their shared yet separate experience. (p. 36)

Slochower's reference to "holding" also refers back to the mother–infant dyad elaborated by Winnicott, developing the nature of that holding as something integral to the therapeutic encounter in which the therapist, in the maternal role, contains the developing synchrony and asynchrony resonating between therapist and patient. Benjamin (2004) refers to "the shared third" in which this particular intersubjective space is "constituted in early, presymbolic experiences of accommodation, mutuality, and the intention to recognise and be recognised by the other" (p. 19). The relational concepts of mutuality and recognition are central to the shared third, as it represents a profound kind of meeting of two subjectivities. In relation to the false self, the shared third comes from the effort to engage spontaneously from true self to true self, something that entails relational risk for both patient and therapist. Thomas needed to feel recognised, not only in the current pain he was experiencing as a result of the contemporary events, but also in the pain (and accompanying shame) of his early life experiences that were coming to the foreground as provoked by the rupture that was created from contemporary events, a rupture that I was able to recognise in its current representation as well as its historical antecedents. Furthermore, Thomas had come to terms with the destruction of his professional persona that had become central to his own idea of his full subjectivity, a function of the foregrounded false self, as discussed in the previous chapter. Thomas and I had come to that place where the analytic whole is the summation of our intersubjectivity in the context of the analytic third. This is the kind of experience that relational psychoanalytic space can offer, an opportunity for the third to emerge and then the potential to see and work through what happens there; the third is the essence of containment.

Throughout the acute period of Thomas's depression and anxiety, the therapeutic task was focused on offering him support by managing the anxiety that was being provoked by the challenging new situation of recovering from the loss of his career (which had been the centre of his life) and adjusting to a period of being unemployed, an experience totally unfamiliar to Thomas. This was a particular challenge for Thomas, as his successful career offered him the perfect stage for his persona (false self) to act upon. When the stage disappeared, his persona was much reduced, leaving him lost and anxious, having to face the real self that had been so accurately kept in the persona's shadow. After some months passed, however, the therapy moved from managing extremes to the regular working through of the relational dynamics of Thomas's life in the context of his depression. A particular relational pattern that we discovered was the vulnerability that Thomas often felt in intimate friendships. He found that when he allowed himself to rely and depend upon someone, they often let him down and were unable to respond to his needs, resulting in relational breakdown. These challenges arose when Thomas felt that the other person in the relationship erected alienating and unexpected boundaries. This pattern of relating was explored and worked over several times during our work together and was obviously a dynamic in our own therapeutic relationship, a relationship that frequently induces feelings of patient dependency and need upon the therapist. There were times, particularly at the start, where my reliance on more conservative interpersonal boundaries in psychotherapy provoked uncomfortable confrontations between us.[18]

One example of this boundary-induced discomfort occurred early on. My consultation room was on the first floor of my building, so, when patients arrived for therapy, I would welcome them in at the street-level entrance to my home and bring them up a flight of stairs to the consultation room to begin their session. When the session was over, I would show them out at the door of the consultation room and let them see themselves downstairs and out. Very early on, Thomas challenged me on this practice. He thought it impolite and did not like what he felt to be a "businesslike" sensibility that he experienced as cold and uncaring, particularly after a session in which he had shared intimate material to which I had responded with obvious care and empathy. We worked through his discomfort around these bound-aries—in short, we were both able to come to understand the meaning of this shutting of boundaries for Thomas. Although I was also able to become more flexible and meet Thomas more gingerly at these bound-aries, they remained a difficult psychic space for us to occupy when they were provoked. I understood what happened at the top of the stairs to be an "enactment", that is, a co-constructed event between the two of us, through which we can understand the patient's material bet-ter. Enactment differs from the more classical understanding of "acting out", which indicates a pathological intrapsychic event solely within the mind of the patient (Roughton, 1995), to the relational perspective where the therapist is a full participant in the event (Slavin & Kreigman, 1998). Hence, Thomas's anger at the top of the steps was not the result of a one-way acting out in which my imposing a "businesslike" bound-ary was the result of his own intrapsychic state, but it was an event that was happening between us partly because of the choices I was making as a therapist and a person. The quintessential factor of relational work lies in just these sorts of enactments. They enable us to understand the relational dynamics activated between therapist and patient, thus allowing them to work through them together. For Thomas and I, the event at the top of the stairs provided both a context for meaning-making and the opportunity to renegotiate our work together, ulti-mately developing a therapeutic idiom that would be uniquely ours. Examples like this helped to show that the psychodynamics that were expressed in Thomas's relationship with me would often resemble ele-ments expressed in relationships with significant others outside the therapy, both historically and contemporaneously. It was the nature of the therapeutic setting (the presence of the third) that allowed us to experience these elements and then understand them that offered the potential for relational growth. The groundwork that we accom-plished here in developing that third space enabled us to endure the coming impingement that threatened to undo all our work.

The virtual impingement

During the second year of therapy, Thomas experienced another intense phase of anxiety stemming from a fast-approaching annual event at his previous place of work in which he would have been crucially involved had he remained there. The prospect of this event evoked the memories of the tragic end to his career that had provoked the re-emergence of latent feelings from his early life that we had begun, through our work, to understand. Our understanding of them, however, did not diminish the impact of Thomas's feelings of anxiety and self-condemnation when they came back with a vengeance. One night, between sessions, Thomas awoke feeling disturbed and anxious, and, unable to go back to sleep, he typed my name into Google and clicked "search". Unconsciously, Thomas was seeking a sense of me, his therapist and "good object", to help him contain these difficult feelings. Disturbingly, the search results produced not the familiar psychotherapist that he thought he knew, but, rather, an unfamiliar story about his therapist's encounter with a venomous insect that had put him in danger. More than that, the story had been shared with tens of thousands of people, across national boundaries—but not shared with Thomas. In a sense, what Thomas had stumbled upon was simply what Google had constructed as an entity in its knowledge graph that stood for me; a simple yet bloated aspect of my cobbled-together online identity. While we can presume that in his search Thomas was unconsciously seeking what he knew of me from our sessions together, what he found was a completely disproportionate representation of me that seemed utterly alien to what he knew of me and felt like a betrayal. Given that Thomas was in a depressed and anxious state, his finding a different object than that which he was seeking was experienced as an intense blow.[19]

The results of Thomas's search appeared in the lonely light cast by his screen in the middle of the night: this was exactly the moment when the virtual impingement occurred *in relation to the two of us*— that is, outside the safety of the consultation room and, therefore, distant from a felt sense of our co-created "third". According to Slochower (2005), it is the analyst's task to hold the "third" for the client, but much of this job is done in the context of the psychotherapy session; Thomas experienced a breach to the third when he was outside the consultation room, where the feelings and fantasies that are provoked can be reality tested on the one hand, and regulated on the other. Benjamin (1988) notes that with mutual recognition comes mutual regulation, too. Much of this mutual regulation is non-verbal and is expressed though the eyes, facial expressions, and other interpersonal cues experienced together, within the third, in the safety of the consultation room, cues that do not exist between an individual and a Google search. For Thomas, this experience occurred outside the confines of the consulting room, at night, during a state of anxiety. Thus was created an impingement. The impingement was experienced as a breach to our "third", resulting in my becoming, in Thomas's mind, an abandoning object rather than a containing one. Thomas, who had shared so much with me, had to find out this global story from a Google search; it was as if I had let thousands of others in, but kept him out. For Thomas, this information about me revealed by a Google search was experienced as an affront. It was an impingement so severe that he experienced it as an offence, an abandonment, and a relational rupture all at the same time. The next day Thomas phoned me, furious and hurt, wanting to terminate the therapy.

While I tried my best to offer containment to Thomas over the phone, a long period followed during which our therapeutic relationship remained tenuous; it certainly did not feel safe enough for Thomas to return without great caution, equivocation, and ambivalence. Although I initially persuaded Thomas to stick with me a bit longer, we had yet to endure several difficult telephone conversations and he regularly threatened to terminate therapy; a return to me as a consistently "good enough" object seemed impossible. All of the work we put into creating that crucial but vulnerable third was burst wide open by a cobbled-together identity offered up by a Google search. Despite this, we plugged away at it. Thomas expressed his hurt, disappointment, and fury towards me. He later confided to me that he had been concerned that this monstrous thing could have hurt me. In the context of Thomas's early life, his intense reaction makes even more sense since he had lost a parent, suddenly, early in his life. His attachment to me had been ambivalent due to his fear of losing another person on whom he could become dependent, and, in a sense, when he found that altered version of me on Google, he felt as if he had lost me, too.[20]

In object relational terms, Thomas's expression of concern for me indicated a positive movement towards what Klein (1935) refers to as the depressive position, in which the fear of the loss of an important object becomes foregrounded rather than the more primitive paranoid–schizoid anxiety, in which he felt as if I had wilfully abandoned him. The shifting back and forth from paranoid–schizoid to depressive positions is a natural and non-pathological dynamic in object relations terms; however, operating from the depressive position indicates progress in the individual's ability to relate to whole rather than part-objects. Because of our previous work together, Thomas was able to reflect that the events happening between us mirrored many of the let-downs and disappointments he had shared with me about his friendships "out there". When our therapeutic relationship had broken down "in here", with the same feelings as those others, it was difficult for him to trust me enough to work it through towards a different end, to take this event that was begging for old-habituated response (abandonment or perceived abandonment) and replace it with a new possibility, that is, to understand this event, like the smaller one at the top of my stairs, as an enactment. Cooper and Levit (2005) describe how enactments draw therapists into the patient's drama:

> Enactments often involve the ways we unconsciously participate in a repetition of an earlier failure that was close to the patient's experience of an earlier trauma (Casement, 1985). The patient is sceptical to believe that the analyst can become a new object partly because the patient sees the ways in which the analyst is the same as the old object through repetition and enactment. (pp. 59–60)

Between Thomas and me, the Google search provoked a relational response towards the old abandoning object, which I then became for Thomas. When this relationship takes hold, it is difficult for the psychotherapist to fully inhabit the new (good) object relationship for the patient, one that can sustain the current rupture. The result is that the enactment takes hold of both parties (both are identified with the old-object relational dynamic); it feels impossible in the heated moment to anchor oneself outside the induced relational tension. When in the grip of an enactment, it is easy for the therapist to lose his or her hold on the "third" because everything becomes alive, electric even, and the "third" seems to fall out of reach. The danger of such enactments is that the patient may not yet have enough trust in the therapist to work through the destructive elements to be able to have that new experience. The revelation of the centipede story struck not only at the heart of Thomas's intrapsychic object-relational dynamics, but also at the centre of our very own relational matrix. The intervention of a centipede, and the chaotic world in which news is collected and forever preserved, presented us with the challenge and the opportunity to work through an impingement that had been arrived at virtually.

Extrapolating themes from the clinic to the wider culture

A Google trail threatens to spread not who one *is* to the observing world, but, instead, a passive online identity: a cobbled-together *representation* of what one is in the clutches of whatever Google has acquired and attached to a name. In the therapeutic situation, this can contaminate the transference by producing disclosure about the therapist that he or she might not have wished to share (see Gorden, 2010). In an important sense, this is nothing new. Aron (1999) distinguishes "self-disclosure" from "self-revelation", which he argues is a continuous process in any case. Psychotherapists self-reveal all the time through their action or inaction, facial expressions, what they choose to respond to and what they do not, even how they choose to see their patients out. Google's disclosures, however, are different, in as much as they occur outside the therapeutic setting and are experienced intrapsychically rather than intersubjectively; there is little containment, little "third" online. This lack of the third intersubjective space can provoke primitive transferences and projections that operate as object-relational phantoms rather than intersubjective phenomena that can be worked through. To be clear, the presence or lack of a third is not solely located in the therapeutic dyad, it operates in some way between any relating individuals; the only difference is that within the analytic dyad the aim is for these things to be made explicit. Each relationship will carry its own idiosyncratic third: different combinations of individuals will also invite their own enactments. These very same relationships, however, are equally vulnerable to virtual impingement when the intersubjective space is mediated online; in the virtual world, they happen all the time. In the therapeutic situation, the question of therapist disclosure, and particularly the loss of power with regard to what a therapist may choose to disclose, is undoubtedly a crucial question for practising clinicians. However, it is precisely because *clinicians are required to ask such questions within the therapeutic context that insights gained there can help shed light on non-therapeutic contexts that are equally vulnerable to virtual impingements.* In other words, contamination of the transference is not a concern for psycho-therapists alone; it prompts consideration of how the virtual world promotes such contamination in the transference of any interpersonal engagement; how online id*entities* come to affect our interpersonal relationships.

The peculiar and specific conditions in which the virtual world impinges on our notion of others and ourselves operate through the same mechanisms I have identified. The therapeutic hour is sensitised not only to *what happens* or *the content or narrative* of events, but also to the potential *unconscious processes* involved in the event in the here-and-now. Thomas was having a reaction to *information about me*, the content of which provoked both his relational repetition (in the trans-ferential sort of way) *and* the dynamics of our unique relational patterning in response to the Google representation of me. In his search, Thomas may have been seeking confirmation of a good, con-sistent object; alternatively, perhaps he was unconsciously searching for the bad, withholding object. We found, through the therapeutic work, that both modes of searching were occurring concurrently. This ambivalence was enacted in our relationship; the consistent, good object was being exchanged for the withholding, bad one in quick succession. The only thing that makes this event special in any way is that there was an opportunity to examine and work through (however difficult that proved to be) the dynamics of the virtual impingement. The presence of psychotherapeutic space is not always available to catch the fallout of these kinds of events that must be happing all the time. The vacillation between the intrapsychic and the intersubjective registers was uncovered only through the therapeutic alliance, which contained just enough third to see us through and help us to under-stand what was happening.

Using material from my experience with Thomas as a guide, we might ask what it is that people may be unconsciously seeking when they search Google for others already known to them. What, indeed, is the motivation? The presumption is that there is *psychological work* being done in the search—but outside the consulting room, how well can this work be processed? Whether there is sufficient thirdness in the virtual world to contain virtual impingements like these is com-pletely dependent on the relational dynamics of the individuals involved alongside the nature or strength of their relationships in the real world. Virtual impingements are not limited to Google searches, they extend to any kind of information-seeking for known or unknown others, or even ourselves, searches occurring outside an intersubjective setting. What is being sought when one is inspecting another's Facebook profile, photo albums, or reading through old status updates? On the relational–unconscious level, the motivations revolve around the desire to discover and to be discovered, orbiting around polarities of narcissistic/exhibitionistic and voyeuristic desires. As is clearly demonstrated by my experience with Thomas, this method of relating is fraught with difficulty when it occurs outside containing relational matrices.

For Thomas and me, understanding both the nature of his motivation *and* our enactment was explicitly part of the task. After many weeks of touch-and-go therapy, we were able to move out of the acute stage of this enactment and start to build safety into the relationship again. In other words, Thomas began to be able to see me as a whole subject again rather than the partial object that had been presented in the Google search. Ultimately, he was also able to see me more fully in my subjectivity, rather than just as an abandoning object. He was able to understand the choices I had made in keeping the story from him, even though he continued to disagree that this was the right approach. In other words, he was able to see the differences between us and found that these differences were not insurmountable. To his ability to contain difference, I credit the relational work we had done together that predated this event—work that gave us both the chance to develop an underlying trust in both the therapeutic process and each other. Ogden (2004) reflects on the enlivening nature of events like this, and the therapeutic importance of such enactments,

> More often than not, I defer interpreting the meanings of such analytic events until much later in the analysis, if I interpret at all. It is living these experiences as opposed to understanding them that is the primary importance to the analysis. (p. 186)

With Thomas, the task was simply to live through the enactment in the best way we could while it was occurring, but it was absolutely crucial that we came to understand it later.

To our ability to contain this enactment I credit the previous idiosyncratic experience of negotiating boundaries together, like those moments of boundary negotiation at the top of my staircase.

Unfortunately, in many non-therapeutic relationships, equally vulnerable to such impingements, there is no such third upon which to rely. With more and more relationships initiated and co-ordinated within virtual spaces (particularly for Digital Natives), this is a grave concern. The good-enough therapeutic relationship is about understanding and working through ruptures like these. However, relationships "out there" that are mediated through social media may not have the foundation that Thomas and I created together to work through the impingement. Furthermore, many of these impingements are also complicated by the fact that they often happen in public: on SNSs it is as if every conversation can and will be overheard. Many online relationships have foundations that either predate or coincide with their online counterparts. However, many do not—such as young people who often elide on- and offline relating—and these relationships are particularly vulnerable to impingements.

Fortunately, Thomas and I were able to work through our virtual impingement. Indeed, eventually we were able to make sense of it and use the experience to deepen the therapy. In fact, the "centipede period" of our therapeutic relationship was something that we would often reflect upon together to make sense of it. Of course, the experience could have caused Thomas to terminate the therapy, undermining all the work we had accomplished up to that point. He could have seen the results on Google, ruminated on it, and never told me: it would have gone on secretly to undermine our relationship implicitly. All of these possibilities are equally available to non-therapeutic relationships encountering virtual impingements. In many ways, it is what might have been seen or known about the other that is *not* expressed that underlies a relationship in even more profound ways, and it is in these ways that such virtual impingements are affecting everyday relationships that have nothing to do with psychotherapy. Gorden (2010) offers a vignette about a Google incursion into the therapeutic setting in which a patient kept the knowledge he acquired about his therapist in a search to himself for some time, creating a dynamic that underlay their relationship for *months* before the fact of the Google search was made known. The result was a sort of prolonged and uncomfortable enactment. She notes that

> [o]ur notions regarding the possibility and achievement of analytic anonymity of our personhood are no longer valid; which of our

patients know about us, what they know, how they know and whether and which parts they disclose to us that they know is no longer something we get to choose. (p. 322)

The way in which the game has changed in relation to our lack of choice with regard to the presence and acquisition of knowledge about us by others is directly applicable outside the analytic setting. What we have all lost is a particular kind of "anonymity", and this loss introduces contamination into the transference of potentially any relationship. The therapeutic space is *ideally* constructed to allow the dyad to work through these kinds of events. However, the dynamics that are evoked in these situations, even if not ideal, can enable us to ask what happens outside the rarefied atmosphere of the consultation room, where the information one obtains from online sources may remain implicit and continue to inform relationships. Object relations has taught us that we have relationships with imagined objects in our minds at least as much as we have them with "real" others. Although the online world has not changed the general psychodynamic processes involved here, it does intervene in the process from quite a different angle. Having information on another, whether true or false, exaggerated or misrepresented, is nothing new; however, the ease with which this information is accessed and the nature by which it is acquired do have noteworthy consequences.

It seems to me that questions are inevitably invited when material of this sort is presented. These revolve around the apparent *newness* of the phenomena. How is information found online any different from information acquired through gossip or hearsay? What about information acquired by other means? In reference to the perspective offered in the Introduction, the response to this question is that the issue here is not about the *content* of the information acquired (although content retains some value), but, rather, that the *process* of seeking information about others is psychological work that is worthy of analysis. Lingiardi (2008) enquired into the psychological meaning of another process, that of patients sending their analysts emails during vacation breaks, and offers four hypotheses in relation to why such emails are sent:

i.   when the fear of losing the object grows
ii. when the patient wants the analyst to recognise parts of her/his self that are still uncertain or too charged with patient or shame-

elements that she/he cannot yet speak about, perhaps, but can already write about;

iii. when the desires associated with transference are frustrated, leading to anger;

iv. When an erotic transference arises, with the anxiety that something can 'happen' during the session. (p. 120)

By utilising a process-orientated approach, we can look for meaning in the unconscious motivation, not simply the content of the result of that motivation. An email can mean any of these things or more, as can the search for a therapist or anyone else on Google. Lingiardi's first hypothesis would equally work for Thomas. His search for me on Google was a process equivalent of another individual's sending of an email. Indeed, all four of Lingiardi's hypotheses, and more, can be applied to online behaviours occurring at any time between individuals outside the clinic. On the more sinister side, the Internet can be used as a way of acting out a whole combination of Lingiardi's hypotheses, as was reported by the writer James Lasdun (2013a), who was cyber-stalked both publicly and privately for years by a former student.[21] The public attacks were Googleable under Lasdun's name, becoming a part of his online identity. Lasdun was forced to ask himself, "Was I going to have to monitor my online pages around the clock? Or would I simply have to accept that this was now going to be a part of my life?" (p. 33). While Lasdun's experience was an extreme, these are questions that most of us will ask ourselves at some point in the future. Everyday, on a more subtle scale, our passive online identities are constructed outside of the will or purpose of the individual subjectivities that these entities come to represent. Yet, the extreme is out there, too, as we will see in Chapter Four, particularly in anonymous forums. It is for these reasons that we need to look more closely at meanings people are making of their online technological lives, not just the content of those lives, material that is covered by so many current studies.

The ease of access to information and the increase in access to others (via email, Twitter, Skype, or whatever) in today's society *enables* enactments to occur without the concomitant psychological work. We operate in a system of such simplicity and convenience that one can search without the consequences of being caught snooping, or send off an email or text message with the click of a button without stopping to think about why. The process remains the same, but the immediacy is different.

Ease and convenience are important issues. As mentioned previously, the kind of information that can be acquired through a few keystrokes, using a search engine, is the same kind of information that previously may have been gained only through physical access to paper records, stalking, or hiring a private detective, a level of commitment that would not only be inhibiting to most, but also the concurrent sense of "going too far" would be palpably correlated to such effort. To be able to enquire without risking consequence (at least in fantasy), at any time of day or night, from any psychological/ emotional position, is also new and noteworthy. These virtual online encounters, outside the intersubjective space of thirdness, ironically create a less "connected up" world, but instead forge one in which object relating takes precedence over subject relating, or what Turkle (2011) calls "the new state of the self, itself":

> When I speak of a new state of the self, itself, I use the word 'itself' with purpose. It captures, although with some hyperbole, my concern that the connected life encourages us to treat those we meet online in something of the same way we treat objects—with dispatch. (p. 168)

What makes the difference between a virtual impingement and one between people is that online interactions are easier to deploy "with dispatch"—that is, quickly, easily, and in an uncontained way: one in which the consequences, too, are experienced from one step of remove. How people use these new tools to negotiate and navigate their ways through their intrapsychic, interpersonal, and social worlds merits further attention. The ease with which we can access information about each other is not without consequence. Seeking out such personal information is psychological work, the distinction being that this psychological work is likely to be operating in isolation. If this is the case, we need to develop an understanding of the processes at play in the context of our connected-up, yet potentially unconnected, culture.

CHAPTER THREE

The matrix

"the electronic age gave us the means of instant total field-awareness. With such awareness, the subliminal life private and social, has been hoicked up into full view"

(McLuhan, 1964, p. 52)

The previous chapter demonstrated how a controlled environment may be utilised to understand, as much as possible, the interpersonal psychodynamics that were provoked by a virtual impingement. The consultation room is a setting in which a variety of external variables are conscientiously muted in the hope that what is left between therapist and patient approaches what might be the closest thing to raw relational data that can then be worked through by way of the therapeutic process. My experience with Thomas showed that, despite all the contrivances put in place to mute these extraneous variables, the therapist's consulting room is not impregnable to impingements (virtual or otherwise): it never really has been. However, the presence of "the third" within the therapeutic holding environment allowed the two of us to work through the dynamics that were found to be operating in response to the impingement. The intersubjective psychodynamics described in both Chapters One and Two have been refined and worked over for more than a century in the continued development of psychoanalytic theory. The application of these refined concepts and understandings from the clinical situation to the social one equally offers us another lens through which we can come to better understand the less conscious aspects of online social networking. Like the consultation room, an individual's relationship to SNSs occurs within a wider context of the larger social matrix that is operating in a highly complex relational environment where all variables are active at once. As online social media is contained within this broader social milieu, we can begin to conceive this matrix as its own kind of holding environment, or container, alongside what we might call an online social third. In this chapter, we leave the consultation room behind, but we take its concepts with us. We turn a psychoanalytic eye not only to the unconscious intersubjective dynamics that underlie interactions across online social networks, but also to how these interactions, through mobile technologies, are now a ubiquitous part of our online and offline realities. In this chapter, we look at the larger ecosystem of technological relating that takes place within the broader socio-cultural system. These interactions are understood to take place within a socio-cultural matrix of online relating.

Between human and machine

From a socio-cultural perspective, it is clear that both individuals and societies attach symbolic meanings to technology and that these meanings forge a co-constructed relationship between society and its technologies. Baym (2010), referring to the work of Sturken and Thomas (2004), notes that what a society says about its technology is as revealing of that society as it is of the technology:

> When we communicate about digital media, we are communicating about ourselves, as individuals, groups, and societies. As we represent these unfamiliar interpersonal tools through our words, conversations, stories, metaphors, images, and so on we collectively negotiate what interpersonal relationships are and what we want them to be. (Baym, 2010, p. 23)

Baym describes this as "reflective" meaning, in that the technology is reflecting something about those that have created and utilise it. Technology is also described as "productive" (Baym, 2010, p. 23) in the sense that the uses of technology change in response to the way in which those technologies are received and utilised within societies; hence, the nature of the relationship between humans and technology is co-constructive.

The way in which technology may be both reflective and productive in the global sense resonates with the dynamic that we have already discussed in the intersubjective domain. The relational perspective highlights the nature of the co-creation of realities that are constructed between individuals in intersubjective space, a perspective that can be extended also to understanding the individual's relationship to their technology and further, working outward to enquire into how societies, and cultures too, interrelate with their technologies. This overall relational approach generates its theory in a dialectical interactive process, one that happens between people, between people and machines, and between those people as they are mediated through machines.

Baym (2010) offers a number of different conceptual tools that can be used to get a handle on the nature of how technology, rather than simply being a passive object of enquiry, is indeed the result of similar interactional dynamics. The model that Baym offers provides a series of perspectives that are in some degree of conflict with each other but that offer a way of making sense of digital media. It is best understood as a series of dialectics between which meaning can be accessed. One perspective is "Technological Determinism" (p. 24) in the sense that "machines change us". This is a rather simplistic and obviously unrelational perspective that can be distilled down into the sentence "the more you use them [technologies], the more they use you, and the more influenced you are by them" (p. 26). Despite the simplicity of this world-view, it is important to understand that it operates as a common trope in the minds of those researching technology, not to mention being a widespread perspective in the media in response to the rapid developments in the sphere of technology and society. Baym notes that this sort of deterministic thinking is prominent in a great deal of research into the effects of technology, studies that measure time spent online, divide people into heavy and light users, or users vs. non-users, and then correlate that measure with outcome variables such as loneliness or time spent with family. What a person was doing online is not addressed, collapsing such diverse activities as keeping in touch with one's mother, banking, researching political information, and looking at pornography into a single causal agent: The Internet. (p. 27)

While there is no doubt that some of these studies can be extremely useful in our understanding of the role that technology has in people's lives, it is also important to remember that most of this research is composed of large-scale quantitative studies that set out to under-stand, nomothetically, what is going on across large groupings of indi-viduals. Furthermore, both these studies and a great deal of the social commentary they foment frequently respond to "the Internet" as a unitary phenomenon rather than the complex system that it is, offer-ing a variety of different possibilities for infinite engagements; they say very little, in fact, about *how individuals themselves understand their particular Internet use.* It is those underlying fundamentals that this book is attempting to address.

In contrast to the technological determinism approach, we find what Baym (2010) terms the "social construction of technology", or SCOT. This perspective lies at the opposite end of the spectrum, whereby technology is theorised to be the result of social processes rather than the other way around. In this perspective, "inventors are embedded in social contexts" (p. 39), meaning that what they produce is not merely a function of what *can* be produced within the limits of materiality or technical curiosity and creativity. Technological development supersedes inventor innovation alone and is inclusive of a variety of other influences, not least the investors, both private and public, who have diverse and often competing goals in response to a vibrant and complex marketplace. The development of the Internet from its initial military and academic purposes to its current form as the global (and mostly open) World Wide Web is a perfect illustration of this as it "exemplifies technology re-envisioned and transformed by users" (Baym, 2010, p. 40). As described in the Introduction, all of the major Internet platforms originated with much less user-friendly interfaces and have evolved to become much more human in their scope. One can simply follow the trajectory of these computer interfaces as they were in the 1980s, when they were under the exclusive domain of programmers and hobbyists, and how they have evolved into intuitive human-friendly technologies exemplified in devices like the iPad and iPhone. Apple, the company that produced these familiar devices, emerged as the first real alternative to the clunky disc operating system (DOS) by offering a mouse through which people interacted with familiar icons (a pointing finger, a manila folder, or the dreaded bomb indicating a system error). It is no accident that the very company that cracked the human–machine interaction problem is currently the most highly valued company in the world: it is now producing phones you can talk to, rather than just through.

The evolution of technology towards a better "fit" with humans lies somewhere between technological determinism and SCOT within the paradigm of what Baym (2010) calls "social shaping", which occupies a middle ground. From this perspective, Baym argues that

> we need to consider how societal circumstances give rise to technologies, what specific possibilities and constraints technologies offer, and actual practices of use as those possibilities and constraints are taken up, rejected and reworked in everyday life. (p. 45)

The social shaping hypothesis, though not explicitly taking up the question of unconscious process and interpersonal psychodynamics, none the less operates on an axiomatic interactional paradigm. The development of the technology itself is relational and one can track a trajectory from a rather clunky inhuman technological beast (think Frankenstein's monster) to an intuitively interactive "made for people" technological world that more closely resembles Data from *Star Trek: The Next Generation*. In fact, examples from popular culture, including Data and the later iteration of a similar technology-wishing-to-be-human holographic doctor *in Star Trek: Voyager*, reflect the changing nature of *both* the human philosophical question of technology in the service of humanity *and* the development of technology towards a state of human *being* itself. In much the same way that the social brain hypothesis suggests that our brains have grown due to the demands of social complexity rather than environmental factors (Dunbar, 1998), we might also suggest that technology is developing in a similar fashion: an outsourced brain being developed to cope with the growing complexity of our social needs. In this sense, the world of social networking becomes an additional virtual resource of the self that enables us to cope with the widening capacity of our growing social ties.

A virtual extension of the self and its consequences

McLuhan (1964) is probably best known for his aphoristic statement, "the medium is the message" (p. 7), and there is little doubt that in the world of online social networking, the message is fully implicated in the media. With an almost disturbing clairvoyant-like perspicacity, McLuhan also stated that

> Today . . . we have extended our central nervous system itself in a global embrace, abolishing both space and time as far as our planet is concerned. Rapidly, we approach the final phase of the extensions of man—the technological simulation of consciousness, when the creative process of knowing will be collectively and corporately extended to the whole of human society, much as we have already extended our senses and our nerves by the various media. (pp. 3–4)

The nature of the extension of our consciousness, and particularly that which is unconscious, is a central tenet of this book. We have already seen how individual subjectivity is already extended outside the self in that it needs to find itself between the intrapsychic world of the self and the intersubjective world of the other: this is accomplished through mutual recognition. McLuhan goes on to ask a question about *the space in-between* that we are continuing to ask of the new media of our own time. McLuhan asks

> Whether the extension of the consciousness, so long sought by advertisers for specific products, will be 'a good thing' is a question that admits of a wide solution. There is little possibility of answering such questions without considering all of them together. Any extension, whether of skin, hand, or foot, affects the whole psychic and social complex. (1964, p. 4)

To call McLuhan "prescient" on this point would be an understatement; his question comes from a time in which electronic media communication was largely one way: from the radio, television, or cinema screen projecting their content on to a relatively passive audience. From today's standpoint, we can safely say that we live in a completely different technological paradigm. To put this in perspective, McLuhan wrote these words not only before the lunar landings, but a full thirteen years before humankind extended beyond the orbit of the Earth by way of the Voyager spacecraft. The computing power aboard this spacecraft, state-of-the-art space-faring technology in 1977, looks positively primitive compared to the hardware you are likely to find in the pocket of the average twelve-year-old today. It seems almost quaint that this height of advancement in the second half of the 1970s carried aboard it a golden phonograph record upon which analogue images have been encoded alongside some "sounds of the earth" on the off chance that aliens will intercept it in interstellar space.[22] When we consider that McLuhan's words pre-date even this advance of "human extension", it serves to remind us that every time we feel that we are on the novel cusp of an epistemic shift in relation to the way humans relate "in a new way" to technology, there is something strangely familiar about yet another iteration of technological change. To each generation, the jump forward feels revolutionary: these advances are developing faster than ever before, making the jump between each generation much shorter. Despite this rapid change, repetition of this sort is somewhat expected in the historic narrative of human beings and their development of tools and technology

Advances that we take for granted today, for example, the writing and recording of words as developed by the ancients, drastically changed the nature of the human society. Naughton (2012a) notes that within the first twenty years after the invention of the Gutenberg Press, medieval citizens would have been unable to predict that it would be a major catalyst in undermining the Catholic Church, triggering the Protestant Reformation and enabling the rise of modern science (p. 13). Naughton positions these major changes in the context of our being within the first twenty years (or so) of the Internet, and wonders if the changes it will bring are as large and unpredictable. The development of technologies like Gutenberg's printing press initiated intense and rapid change in which, Carr (2010) notes, "the number of books produced in the fifty years following Gutenberg's invention equalled the number produced by European scribes during the preceding thousand years" (p. 69). The invention of the printing press enabled an explosion in the availability of written materials, causing a massive drop in price, democratising access to information as in no time preceding it. Compare this to a report by Short, Bohn, and Baru (2011) which found that

> In 2008, the world's servers processed 9.57 zettabytes of information, almost 10 to the 22nd power, or ten million million gigabytes. This was 12 gigabytes of information daily of the average worker, or about 3 terabytes of information per worker per year. (p. 7)

While both the impenetrable jargon used and the sheer size of the numbers make this finding intellectually ungraspable to most, Eric Schmidt (CEO at Google) famously put it in perspective by claiming "There were five exabytes of information created between the dawn of civilisation through 2003, but that much information is now created every two days, and the pace is increasing" (M. Kirkpatrick, 2010). Although some dispute Mr Schmidt's statement on the basis that he was not including copied and repeated information, which makes up a rather great deal of today's digital production through the sheer ease of simplicity of replication, even so, it is mind-boggling. Gutenberg's press equally will have produced more repeated information than new information (indeed, this was the point); it is the repetition and the scale of access that made the invention such a paradigm shifter. Comparing the paradigm changing Web 2.0 to the Gutenberg press is not an understatement. The sociologist Christakis (2010) compares the "mind expanding" nature of the Internet with earlier "brain enhancing" technologies, in which he includes the printing press and the telephone; however, he maintains that this does not essentially change us in a substantial way: in using the word "essentially", Christakis is referring to our brains. Noting that human group sizes have not changed at all since Roman times (he provides evidence of this by looking at the size of military units, which, he tells us, have not changed substantially in size in over 2000 years), Christakis concludes that our brains continue to work in relation to Dunbar's number (about 150),[23] tracking social relationships "to form mental rosters that identify who is who, and to form mental maps that track who is connected to whom and how strong or weak, or cooperative or adversarial, those relationships". Christakis reminds us that while social networks like Facebook may use the word "friends" to label the

scores, hundreds, or thousands of contacts we have across that particular network, "they are decidedly not our friends, in the truly social,
emotional, or biological sense of the word"; the Internet is not "changing our fundamental proclivity to violence or our innate capacity for
love". For Christakis, then, social networking operates quite simply as
a tool (much as the printing press or the telephone) that does not, in
the end, alter us in any fundamental way, it merely keeps our "contacts" in a particular network in order. As we shall see in the following chapters, Christakis is incorrect in categorising online friendships
as he does, in that not all friends across SNSs are treated the same
way. Rather, close friends, acquaintances, and strangers are handled
and conceived of differently across SNSs, as they are in real life.

Not all theorists and researchers agree that as our engagement
with social networking grows, our brains remain unchanged. Carr
(2010) cites research with primates carried out by Ultima and colleagues (2008) in which monkeys were taught how to use tools such
as rakes and pliers to acquire food. The study found that

> the rakes and pliers actually came to be incorporated into the brain
> maps of the animals' hands. The tools, so far as the animals' brains
> were concerned, had become part of their bodies ... the monkeys'
> brains began to act 'as if the pliers were now the hand fingers'. (cited
> in Carr, 2010, p. 32)

If we conceive of the Internet as the tool that it most certainly is, then
break it down further to see how online social networking is a tool
that is used explicitly for the presentation of self and social relating,
the consequences for our brain, and even the evolution of our species,
is potentially immense. Researchers from a variety of different perspectives are finding brain changes in relation to the Internet, from the
preliminary findings by Small, Moody, Siddarth, and Bookheimer
(2009) on the potential positive effects of Google searching on older
people's brains to a study by Kühn et al. (2011), who found brain
changes in the fMRI scans of high frequency video-game-using
adolescents that were similar to those found in relation to addiction.
There are hundreds of such studies that are making links between the
usage of technology and brain changes. Carr (2010) worries that the
expansion of our consciousness into the Internet is not a neutral one
and warns that the ways in which we engage through it have some
worrying consequences that he refers to as a "shallowing":

when we go online we enter an environment that promotes cursory reading, hurried and distracted thinking, and superficial learning. It's possible to think deeply while surfing the Net, just as it's possible to think shallowly while reading a book, but that's not the type of thinking the technology encourages and rewards . . . if, knowing what we know today about the brain's plasticity, you were to set out to invent a medium that would rewire our mental circuits as quickly and thoroughly as possible, you would probably end up designing something that looks and works a lot like the Internet. It's not just that we tend to use the Net regularly, even obsessively. It's that the Net delivers precisely the kind of sensory and cognitive stimuli—repetitive, intensive, interactive, addictive—that have been shown to result in strong and rapid alterations in brain circuits and functions . . . the Net may well be the single most powerful mind-altering technology that has ever come into general use. (Carr, 2010, pp. 115–116)

The way in which Carr is referring to the effects of technology on the human being here is in many ways indicative of the "technological determinism" approach that Baym described above. In Carr's description, we can see how the technology is theorised to operate upon us in a singular, damaging way, rather than potentially developing in conversation with human needs and desires. From an evolutionary perspective, we can see how human needs and desires continue to be motivated by more primitive imperatives that are expressed within a world that has evolved technologically at great speed while our primary motivations have stayed largely the same. There is a whole variety of tasks that our brains have evolved to do that technology challenges in a number of ways: one such example is the way in which the brain operates between working memory and long-term memory. Carr (2010) draws a simple schema for us to understand the relationship between the two: "If working memory is the mind's scratch pad, then long-term memory is its filing system" (p. 123). Working memory, however, can only operate effectively with a small number (between about two and seven) of chunks of information at a time. Carr argues that the way in which we are exposed to fast-moving information today is influencing this process of working memory to long-term memory. The Internet operates in a way that can expose us to too much cognitive load, which interferes with the working memory and makes it difficult for information being absorbed in the working memory to be transmitted into the long-term memory. Carr (2010) uses the handy image of filling a bathtub (long-term memory) with a thimble (short-term memory):

> By regulating the velocity and intensity of information flow, media exert a strong influence on this process. When we read a book, the information faucet provides a steady drip, which we can control by the pace of our reading. Through our single minded concentration on the text, we can transfer all or most of the information, thimbleful by thimbleful, into long-term memory ... With the Net, we face many information faucets, all going full blast. Our little thimble overflows as we rush from one faucet to the next. We're able to transfer only a small portion of the information to long-term memory, and what we do transfer is a thimble of drops from different faucets, not a continuous, coherent stream from one source. (pp. 124–125)

The difference between the way in which we might read and absorb the information from a book and the over-determined ways in which we engage with the Internet invite a series of consequences for the way in which we do or do not process information. Emotional content, too, is information; it just operates on a different register than the cognitive abilities required for the information to which Carr refers. In psychotherapy, similarly, we have an understanding of what kind of psychological or emotional load can be assimilated at any one time: for example, post traumatic stress disorder [PTSD] is seen to be a result of a trauma in which an individual has been overstimulated with emotional material. Psychotherapists are trained to "titrate" their engagement with a patient so as not to overwhelm them with their interventions. Under-titrating risks the patient feeling that they are not being adequately responded to, while over-titration can cause anxiety, flooding, and emotional overload. Titration can only be deployed properly in the context of an intersubjective space where both subjects are mutually attuned and regulate each other by maintaining awareness of each other's subjectivities (Benjamin, 1988) to ensure that both parties are "with each other" during the exchange. While Carr is not, in this case, interested in emotional information, the model he offers with regard to the velocity and intensity of data can, none the less, be applied to the emotional register.

The way in which the Internet offers faucets (to use Carr's language) instead of pipettes (to use mine) may have a similar effect on our relational systems as it does on our memory systems, potentially causing disruption in that system between our responses to the multiple faucets continually demanding our attention online and the deep relational structures from which our motivation to relate emerges in the first place. Cyber-theorist Stone (2012) has coined the phrase "continuous partial attention" to describe what Carr has linked to working and long-term memory in a similar dynamic for relational systems:

> To pay continuous partial attention is to pay partial attention—CONTINUOUSLY . . . Another way of saying this is that we want to connect and be connected. We want to effectively scan for opportunity and optimize for the best opportunities, activities, and contacts, in any given moment. To be busy, to be connected, is to be alive, *to be recognized*, and to matter. We pay continuous partial attention in an effort NOT TO MISS ANYTHING. It is an always-on, anywhere, anytime, any place behavior that involves an artificial sense of constant crisis. We are always in high alert when we pay continuous partial attention. This artificial sense of constant crisis is more typical of continuous partial attention than it is of multi-tasking. (my italics)

There is a familiarity in the way that Stone describes this phenomena of continuous partial attention; it sounds like a controversial psychopathology that we are all too familiar with, and one that is becoming a seemingly ubiquitous condition, attention deficit/hyperactivity disorder (ADHD), which is characterised by the *DSM-IV-TR* as "a persistent pattern of inattention and/or hyperactivity-impulsivity" (American Psychiatric Association, 2000, p. 85) and which can be diagnosed if an individual has six or more of the following symptoms of inattention lasting for at least six months "to a degree that is maladaptive and inconsistent with developmental level":

a. often fails to give close attention to details or makes careless mistakes in schoolwork, work or other activities
b. often has difficulty sustaining attention in tasks or play activities
c. often does not seem to listen when spoken to directly
d. often does not follow through on instructions and fails to finish school work, chores, or duties in the workplace . . .
e. often has difficulty organizing tasks and activities
f. often avoids, dislikes, or is reluctant to engage in tasks that require sustained mental effort . . .
g. often loses things necessary for tasks or activities . . .
h. is often easily distracted by extraneous stimuli
i. is often forgetful of daily activities. (p. 92)

Few people who spend a great deal of time on the Internet will not be able to identify with many of these criteria or, at the very least, be able to identify scores of other people who exhibit many of them. The degree to which these criteria may be "maladaptive and inconsistent with developmental level" may be changing as society as a whole seems to be more and more liable to exhibit these behaviours. Cascio (2009) conflates Stone's idea of continuous partial attention with attention deficit disorder (ADD) and states that we are experiencing "an induced form of ADD—a 'continuous partial attention-deficit disorder,' if you will". From these varying perspectives, we can see why Carr (2010), as quoted above, worries about the "single most powerful mind-changing technology that has ever come into general use" (p. 116). With reference to the experiments that led him to create the thimble–bathtub metaphor, Carr warns that they "indicate that as we reach the limits of our working memory, it becomes harder to distinguish relevant information from irrelevant information, signal from noise. We become mindless consumers of data" (p. 135). With regard to information overload, being able to distinguish the signal from the noise is obviously essential, particularly in a world that continues to produce so much noise; this is as relevant for the emotional as for the cognitive register of information content. The experiments that Carr is referring to do not ask questions about how individuals relate to others via online social networking, yet his concerns with regard to information overload, over-titration, and the signal being lost in the noise are all relevant to the question of relationality in the face of technologies. While it would be foolish to map one series of research findings on to a separate research question, we can still utilise the dynamics inherent in these findings and apply them obliquely to the question of human relating, at the very least in the form of the questions we ask. Such questions would include:

- What is the nature of technological mediation (or interference) on the way in which humans are relating to each other over its networks?
- How does the architecture of SNSs affect the way in which we seek and give recognition?
- How does modern technology interact with our primitive motivations to relate to others?

These questions seek out that boundary between the technological determinism paradigm, which, no doubt, exerts some force, and that of the social shaping paradigm, which clearly implicates human users in relation to their technologies by asking what processes are going on between them as our social lives become more and more entwined online. This entwinement is increasing apace with a new generation of smartphones linking up to 4G networks, guaranteeing that being online on the go can be just as fast as a high-speed broadband connection. Furthermore, as SNSs develop to become more mobile friendly, mobile interaction occurs more and more outside the home. Between 2011 and 2012, time spent by consumers on social applications by way of their mobile phones grew by seventy-six per cent (Neilsen, 2012, p. 5) Twitter, for example, has experienced explosive growth due to its micro-blogging architecture, which works so synergistically with mobile devices; it is as if Twitter were made for mobile devices which allow people to engage piecemeal on the go. The growth of Twitter usage is particularly high among young people:

> Twitter usage is highly correlated with the use of mobile technologies, especially smartphones. One in five smartphone owners (20%) are Twitter users . . . Indeed this correlation between Twitter adoption and smartphone ownership may help to explain the recent growth in Twitter usage among young adults. Those aged 18–24 are not just the fastest growing group when it comes to Twitter adoption over the last year—they have also experienced the largest increase in smartphone ownership of any demographic group over this same period of time. (Smith & Brenner, 2012, p. 5)

The growth in smartphone take-up has had a similar effect for photo sharing platforms such as Instagram and others that allow individuals to "check in" at a variety of locations (e.g., restaurants, parks, bars, etc.) and broadcast this check-in across a variety of SNSs. More than ever before, our online relating has become ubiquitous.

Ubiquity

The ubiquity and connectivity of the smartphone now means that people can be connected all of the time. Ofcom (2011) reports that ninety-three per cent of UK adults had a personal mobile phone in

2011, twenty-seven per cent of those phones were smartphones, and for young people it is about half. We can assume that today, in 2013, this number is growing even higher as prices come down and people continue to renew contracts and upgrade from traditional mobile phones to smartphones. Nearly a quarter of young people with smartphones are reporting that they are watching less television and fifteen per cent are reading fewer books, which indirectly indicates that their attention is being held more and more by these devices. Such phones are becoming a constant companion:

> The vast majority of smartphone users (81 per cent) have their mobile switched on all of the time, even when they are in bed, with four in ten adults (38 per cent) and teens (40 per cent) admitting using their smartphone after it woke them.
>
> Over half (51 per cent) of adults and two thirds (65 per cent) of teenagers say they have used their smartphone while socialising with others, nearly a quarter (23 per cent) of adults and a third (34 per cent) of teenagers have used them during mealtimes and over a fifth (22 per cent) of adult and nearly half (47 per cent) of teenage smartphone users admitted using or answering their handset in the bathroom or toilet. (Ofcom, 2011)

The information above comes from the Ofcom report entitled "A nation addicted to smartphones", a title that clearly indicates the symbiotic relationship that smartphone users are developing with their devices, a symbiosis that seems to be infringing on real-life relational time, which may have some disturbing consequences for home and relational life. When we apply Carr's thinking about the potential nature of tools becoming an aspect of the biological mapping of our brains, it starts to become clear that, as a society, we are extending ourselves into the virtual world through the devices we keep in our pockets. Turkle's (2011) research seems to validate Carr's thinking, in that her subjects are reporting that their mobile devices are indeed becoming a (sometimes unwanted) part of their psychic space that "eat away at their time to think":

> One [subject] says, 'I don't have enough time alone with my mind.' Others say, 'I have to struggle to make time to think.' 'I artificially make time to think.' 'I block out time to think.' These formulations all depend on an 'I' imagined as separate from the technology, a self that

is able to put the technology aside so that it can function independently of its demands. This formulation contrasts with a growing reality of lives lived in the continuous presence of screens. (p. 167)

More and more, it seems that it is indeed becoming a task to remove oneself from the ubiquity of screen-based connection: rather than opting in, it seems more a matter of opting out. According to a recent report by Google (2012), Americans spent 4.4 hours *of leisure time* each day in front of screens (p. 8) and 38% of media time takes place on smartphones, of which 54% of *that* time is used for communication. The report goes on to describe what it calls "multi-screening", which is divided into two sorts of use; sequential "moving from one device to another" or simultaneous "using more than one device at the same time" (p. 17). This research is pointing towards a norm in which attention is continually divided between three main combinations of smartphone–TV, smartphone–PC and PC–TV with a full 78% of the time being devoted to multi-tasking (p. 27). Simultaneous multi-screening is frequently a social affair and eighty-one per cent of simultaneous multi-screening occurs between a television and a smartphone (Google, 2012, p. 25). According to Neilsen,

> Having a mobile device on-hand while watching TV has become an integral part of consumer routines—41 per cent of tablet owners and 38 per cent of smartphone owners use their device daily in front of their TV screen . . . social networking is a top activity on both devices. (p. 13)

Just a couple of years ago, when "on demand" TV was gaining in popularity, social commentators were decrying the death of national "water cooler" moments in response to major televisual events. Today, the water cooler has been exchanged for the hashtag. Twitter enables a national conversation that can be followed by *anyone* simply by commenting on a hashtag (e.g., #questiontime or #thearchers), while on Facebook individuals share the experience with a closer network of friends. The art of paying singular attention to one source of media appears to be dying, but this is bringing other benefits, such as social sharing. Nevertheless, these developments pose the question of whether there are similar consequences with regard to divided attention for interpersonal relationships.

Although Google's (2012) research does not directly help us to answer this question, it does none the less open up a window and show us the inside of a ubiquitous online world where attention is almost always divided. These developments are having consequences for individual subjectivities as well as within the nature of an individual's relationships with others in the real world, not just the virtual one. The function of ubiquity results in people choosing to connect with technology even when in the company of real others. Turkle (2011) describes the effect of mobile devices on interpersonal relationships in the way that they have made each of us "pausable":

> Our face-to-face conversations are routinely interrupted by incoming calls and text messages . . . in the new etiquette, turning away from those in front of you to answer a mobile phone or respond to a text has become close to the norm. When someone holds a phone, it can be hard to know if you have that person's attention. A parent, partner, or child glances down and is lost to another place, often without realizing that they have taken leave. (p. 161)

This "pausability" goes beyond texting and mobile technologies and extends to a whole variety of synchronous online and digital textual communications from BlackBerry Messaging (BBM) through to Skype and Facebook messaging. The nature of online textual communication, because it often occurs when one is multi-tasking, results in conversations being picked up and dropped with frustrating frequency. It has become a norm that a conversation started on Facebook messenger may suddenly stop, perhaps because someone's boss has come into the room, or the phone has rung. What develops is an underlying system of communication in which each party not only expects that they might be dropped, but has come to accept it as a natural component of online and mobile communications. We have not only become pausable, we have become droppable as well. Turkle notes a study (Ophir, Nass, & Wagner, 2009) that indicates that everything we do while multi-tasking degrades the quality of the tasks at hand; this no doubt includes relating. In this case, it is not necessarily the online social networks themselves that are the problem, but the combination of their ubiquity and accessibility. Seligman (2009) notes that "[t]ime that was previously spent interacting socially is increasingly been [sic] displaced by the virtual variety" (p. 15). What might be the reason for a tuning out of face-to-face relating for the purposes of online relating? One suggestion might be that online relating can offer a quick fix. To carry on the eating metaphor from Chapter One, this ease of social interaction by way of the immediate and virtual is indeed like eating a doughnut—satisfying, of course, but is it nourishing?

In a similar vein, Hofmann notes that the "cost" of virtual engagement can seem invisible compared to other enticing and addictive substances, such as cigarettes or alcohol. In response to research that Hofmann and his team carried out in relation to the addictive quality of checking social and other media (such as Twitter and email), Hofmann told *The Guardian* that:

> Desires for media may be comparatively harder to resist because of their high availability and also because it feels like it does not 'cost much' to engage in these activities, even though one wants to resist . . . With cigarettes and alcohol there are more costs – long-term as well as monetary – and the opportunity may not always be the right one. So, even though giving in to media desires is certainly less consequential, the frequent use may still 'steal' a lot of people's time. (Meikle, 2012)

Hofmann is drawing the connection here between ubiquity, convenience, and the lack of a tangible negative reinforcement in the face of the attention that ubiquitous online interaction attracts. The growing social acceptability of managing mobile devices in social environments is removing the stigma that would normally operate as a negative incentive; the negative consequences of this kind of divided attention for face-to-face real-life relationships are likely to be cumulative and only become apparent over time. They can operate like the insidious but completely undramatic signals that, over time, bring an end to a relationship. Turkle (2011) notes that while multi-tasking results in each of the tasks in which one is engaged are done less well, there is, none the less, a benefit:

> multitasking feels good because the body rewards it with neurochemicals that induce a multitasking 'high.' The high deceives multitaskers into thinking they are being especially productive. In search of the high, they want to do even more . . . we fell in love with what technology made easy. Our bodies colluded. (p. 163)

Concomitant with this high is, no doubt, a relational high that results from the excitement of being called upon through the mobile device. A ping on a telephone that says to an individual: "somebody is think-ing of YOU"—despite the fact that this individual may already be engaged in a real-life relational encounter with another person. The same is true if a mobile phone is set to issue a signal when one has been engaged with on Facebook or Twitter. The attention that is drawn to the pinging device offers an attraction that compels the indi-vidual to check their device: it is "relational-lite".

What relational-lite provides is a paradigm in which connection is always available at the tips of one's fingers, and I mean this literally. As we have seen, this can offer some potential disruptions for sus-tained attention with regard to being with a relational "other", but it also has consequences for being alone. Chapter One detailed how good-enough mutual recognition offers a chance for the psyche to develop holistically, enabling healthy development of a complete self that is loved and maintained in the mind of the other. Paradoxically, it also enables what Winnicott (1982c) refers to as "the capacity to be alone". Given that there has been good-enough mothering and a posi-tive facilitating environment, the growing child develops a capacity in which "the ego-supportive environment is introjected and built into the individual's personality, so that there comes about a capacity to actually be alone" (p. 36). In simpler words, the child develops a sense of trust that things are all right when he is alone because he has inter-nalised the supportive love of his primary care-taker in a way that is sustaining, even when that care-taker is no longer there. If the facili-tating environment has not been good-enough (if it has been condi-tional, for example), the child may develop an over-reliance on the false self, or persona, in which case the capacity to be alone is dimin-ished as the false self and persona both require a particular kind of gaze from the outside in order to thrive. One example of the kind of relational pathology that can result from this variation of the facilitat-ing environment is narcissism, which will be discussed more fully in the following chapter. In narcissism, this gaze, because it falls upon the false self, is never felt by the real self of its recipient to "fill the cup", and, hence, more and more of the approving gaze of the other is sought. Some of the major aspects of SNSs enable this insatiable need for topping-up to continue unabated; mobile technologies then extend this even further into just about every reach of daily life. The double-edgedness of SNS and smartphone ubiquity is felt clearly here—it enables contact while, at the same time, offering a dizzying array of distractions from this contact. Furthermore, the ever presence of "relational-lite" distractions enables individuals to avoid instances when they would otherwise experience moments of aloneness, arguably deteriorating their ability to be alone without distraction. One wonders whether the ubiquity of social networking is the new opiate of the masses.

The capacity to be alone naturally emerges from the experience of a facilitating environment that comes complete with absences and frustrations in which the infant develops a way to sustain herself. By way of optimal frustration (the non-ideal but non-neglectful attention paid by the primary care-taker), the infant learns to deal with absence without falling apart. In object relations terms, she develops sustainable internal objects that enable her to cohere as an integrated ego—to remain whole and all right in the face of these absences. From the contemporary relational perspective, this capacity also allows the infant to deal with difference when the care-taker is present. In today's environment, the opportunity to practise being alone appears to be available less and less. Turkle (2011) notes that the ubiquity of mobile phones (not to mention smartphones) enables what she calls "tethering", which she proposes is of particular concern to young people who may lack the chance to develop a sense of being on their own:

> the tethered child does not have the experience of being alone with only him- or herself to count on. For example, there used to be a point for an urban child, an important moment, when there was a first time that they were on their own and responsible. If they were frightened, they had to experience those feelings. The cell phone buffers this moment. (p. 173)

This notion of buffering can be extrapolated right out across the matrix and the way our society is today tethered to technology as a salve to moments of aloneness, relational anxiety, and the experience of difference. The constant availability of relational distraction is there to take the edge off being with one's self.

While tethering has consequences for us all, there are other considerations that come to bear when we consider the difference between Digital Natives and Digital Immigrants. As a Digital Immigrant myself, I remember my younger days when I left home to travel across

Europe by train, the days before mobile phones found their way into the pockets of the general public. Generations of young people like me were taking to the continent's railways and would often go weeks without checking in at home. There was a certain freedom in being released into a foreign country with only one's wits to rely on, and the occasional checking in at home by way of a calling card from a public telephone. This period of time was, for many in my generation, an important period of post-adolescent separation and individuation, and the testing of the capacity to be alone. Turkle (2011) reminds us that it is not only young people who may be suffering a loss here, but parents, too. She notes how parents who give their children mobile phones carry the expectation that their children will answer their calls and experience anxiety when they do not. One member of her study, a mother of four, noted,

> "I envy my mother. We left for school in the morning. We came home. She worked. She came back, say at six. She didn't worry. I end up imploring my children to answer my every message. Not because I feel I have a right to their instant response. Just out of compassion [for my own anxiety]." (p. 174)

The ubiquity of mobile, eternally connected-up technology has invited new anxieties when previously there were none. If you do not believe me, how did you feel when your broadband connection last went down for half an hour?

Technological ubiquity has indeed offered a great deal of opportunity, but at the same time it has connected us in an embrace that might feel too tight, a fibre-optic umbilical cord that retains the capacity to strangle. Ubiquitous connected-up instantaneous culture has produced a dynamic system in which our internal object relations themselves are outsourced. Before a moment is left to be one's own, one is connected to others. While some forms of this online connection are indeed beneficial, there are others that may get in the way of other capacities, such as the capacity to be alone. In this way, the pinging of the phone in the pocket that either disrupts face-to-face intersubjectivity or aloneness is indeed very much like fast food. The more challenging engagements which may be compared to chewing the vegetables, or even enjoying the complexities of a large and varied meal, are set aside for MSG laden snacks that hit the spot, quickly, but may lack depth and sustenance.

CHAPTER FOUR

Who's afraid of being an object?

"I'm your only friend
I'm not your only friend
But I'm a little glowing friend
But really I'm not actually your friend"

(They Might Be Giants, 1990)

A ll SNSs were not created equally; as we have seen, the turn-over of the SNS from one faddish iteration to the next seems now to be slowing, and today (mid 2013) Facebook is by far the most dominant SNS on the planet with an online population of around one billion people (Facebook, 2012b). Five years ago, Ofcom (2008) reported that half of their UK respondents had a MySpace profile; today Myspace's demise is illustrated in its fall in global website ranking to the 208th most visited site, according to Alexa (2012), compared to Facebook occupying the number two slot, just behind Google's search engine, making it the most visited social network on the Internet. In the UK, there are a variety of variables that attract a certain kind of user to a given social network, most notably, age and, to a lesser degree, class (Ofcom, 2008). Facebook's success in its transnational colonisation (Swift, 2012) supports McLuhan's (1964) prediction that "we approach the final phase of the extensions of man—technological stimulation of consciousness, when the creative process of knowing will be collectively and corporately extended to the whole of human society" (p. 3). Although all of the hype and anticipation that Facebook would be as financially successful as its popularity would suggest were dashed when its shares rapidly declined after its IPO. By mid 2013 it shares had mostly recovered, though they are expected to remain volatile. *The Economist's* (2011) optimistic claim that "The only area of business that seems to be recession-proof is social media" may not have been misguided after all. Whatever happens to its shares in the short term, however, is in no way indicative of Facebook's success in functioning as a social platform; in fact, the way in which it has historically been difficult to monetise is actually a point of interest. Is it that, as a primarily *social* network, it resists, in some inherent way, the monetising and objectifying of its users for market purposes? Perhaps Google is enormously more effective with advertisers than Facebook because people go to Google, amongst other things, to search for things to buy, but go to Facebook in order to socialise with each other. If Benjamin (1988) is right that the primary human motivation is to seek and be sought and to recognise and be recognised, then the marketer's desire to make consuming objects out of socialising subjects has been a rather difficult route to plan by way of the SNS. Still, Facebook's investors continue to look for ways to exploit their massive captive audience to better use the platform to create profit. One of the ways this is developing is through Facebook's "ecosystem", the way in which the social network grows and colonises an individual's online activity far beyond interacting with friends through basic text based messaging systems. This is exemplified in Facebook's 2012 purchase of the popular photography application Instagram, an application that enables individuals to take pictures on the move and share them with friends. Shortly after its purchase, Instagram changed its terms and conditions to allow it to use "any or all of . . . [a user's personal] photographs for advertising and other purposes, at its sole discretion" (Naughton, 2012b, p. 27). In reflecting on this development in the *Observer's* Comment section, Naughton wryly reminds us of "the old Internet adage 'if the service is free than you are the product'". If there is any indication that the world's largest online social networking site is trying to make a commercial object out of human subjects, this is certainly one of them.

Nowadays, everything is social

The broad strategy here is that by way of its ecosystem, Facebook will become more and more of a portal through which individuals engage in a variety of online activities that are not explicitly about socialising, instead, they sit atop a foundation that is composed of interpersonal engagement. Much more than just a place to connect with friends via wall posting and photo sharing, Facebook is seen to be a "social utility . . . which lets people do all kinds of things, from passing on newspaper articles to playing games or posting photos of themselves" while expanding further by allowing outside developers to create apps that seamlessly integrate with the social sharing experience (*The Economist*, 2012). This seamless integration begins to break down the implicit boundaries we have historically had between what is private and what is public, not only in the blatantly commercial ways as demonstrated by Instagram, but in more subtle ways as well. For example, whereas reading a newspaper used to be a relatively private activity, nowadays if you happen to read it online, by way of a link suggested by a Facebook friend, you will find that your "friends" are seeing what you have read alongside who suggested it to you, too. While this is easily avoided by finding the link through another window in your browser, the *ease and convenience* of clicking a link that appears ready on your homepage is irresistible to most, and this is the very point. The same is true for the music you may be listening to through a similar application.

In the scheme of things, this is no bad thing. You are likely to have much in common with your Facebook friends, and they are a great source of sharing material of mutual interest. This is, indeed, the "in" for advertisers: to highly select the ads that will be displayed based on your tastes. For advertisers as well as many consumers, this is a real boon, since a one size fits all approach to advertising might be on the way out; consumers will be introduced to products which they are likely to be interested in buying. Advertising, *per se*, is not the problem here, the problem lies in the collocation of advertising and social sharing alongside the ease and convenience with which previously private operations have become public ones: this has implications not only for privacy, but also upon how we interact as complex subjects.

As these choices that we make while alone in front of our computers become public acts, individuals become more aware of their public-facing selves and the previously private activities start operating in the domain of the persona and false self. Whereas reading an article may have previously been an exercise of self-edification, it now comes with the incentive for social bragging or the potential cost of social judgement. As Wilcox and Stephen (2012) point out

> people use social networks to fulfil a variety of social needs, including affiliation, self-expression, and self-presentation . . . when adolescents receive positive feedback on their social network profile, it enhances their self esteem and well being. (section on self-presentation, par. 2)

The expanding nature of the Facebook ecosystem is enforcing a conflation of private and public desires. When outward-facing ego needs such as self-expression and self-presentation are conflated with private ego needs such as self-development and recreation, the result is an intrusion of the false-self domain into the true-self domain. While an individual might be comfortable sharing a given popular music track or article from a newspaper that reflects the political values or social point of view of their social network, they may be rather less amenable to sharing music they know their friends might scoff at or an article that betrays a less acceptable political perspective. What begins to develop after a series of these decisions is a reliance on recognition of the false self that develops in relation to the desired self-presentation for a given audience.

The presence of what boyd (2007) terms "imagined audiences" has become central to the online social networking experience. The concept of internal objects is not dissimilar to boyd's notion of imagined audiences, in that both operations are about the internalised witnessing of the self by a kind of imagined gaze of the other. For Freud, this witnessing occurs as a dynamic between the superego and the ego; in the object relations tradition, the internal witnessing of the self (or, more specifically, aspects of the self) comes by way of the multiple introjected objects gained from original relationships. A combination of character and the nature of these early relationships will determine the quality of the internal object relationships. These internal object relations are then projected outward, and the ideas of one's imagined audiences will be based upon these projections to some degree. Another way of looking at this comes through the work of sociologists Riesman, Glazer, and Denny (1950) on the "other directed self", in which people look towards others for validation. Turkle (2011) develops their ideas in relation to technology, terming a new kind of "hyper-other-directedness" in which

> . . . other-directedness is raised to a higher power. At the moment of beginning to have a thought or feeling, we can have it validated, almost pre-validated. Exchanges may be brief, but more is not necessarily desired. The necessity is to have someone there. (p. 177)

The widening of social sharing, together with the platform-side advantages of using social sharing to advertise, works synergistically here to shift user attention to imagined audiences and other-directedness. These relations are dependent on what boyd (2007) refers to as "networked publics", which are distinguished from private publics and defined as "the spaces and audiences that are bound together through technological networks (i.e. the Internet, mobile network, etc.). Networked publics are one type of *mediated public*; the network mediates the interactions between members of the public" (p. 8). The functions of being a subject within a networked public, though essentially relational and intersubjective, is dependent upon imagined audiences because the "other" is always at some distance; naturally, this invokes more projection based on internal object relations than face-to-face relating does.

The development of social applications increases the colonial aspect of SNSs such as Facebook by allowing them to become a one-stop online shop where any online activity can be accessed through the SNS's interface. With regard to Facebook, "These are all part of its ambitious plan to map all of the connections between people and the things that interest them" (*The Economist*, 2012). This "ambitious plan" will be developed, no doubt, in response to a variety of influences, not least the commercial interests of its investors since becoming public. In the context of Facebook's financial troubles at the time, prolific blogger Brian Solis (2012) notes the reasons that Facebook was not initially created to be a profit-making company:

It was built to accomplish a social mission—to make the world more open and connected. The social network hopes to strengthen how people relate to each other. Even though Facebook's mission sounds big, the company is focusing on starting small—with the relationship between two people. Its focus is building tools to help people connect with the people they want and share what they want, and by doing this they are extending people's capacity to build and maintain relationships.

No doubt Facebook's ambitions have grown since becoming a public company. Its development in this direction is a good illustration of the social-shaping hypothesis discussed in the previous chapter. It also represents an ironic about-face with regard to the development of Web 2.0, which developed its interactive capacity initially to allow for financial transactions to be made online with ease (Naughton, 2012a). As discussed earlier, this interaction opened up the road for Web 2.0's massive social interactionism, which is now trying itself to become as financially feasible as the buying of books and T-shirts. Facebook, which started out as the Harvard-only, tongue-in-cheek "Facemash", an expression of Zuckerberg's "rebellious irreverent side" (D. Kirkpatrick, 2010), has now become the world's most dominant social network in response to both the social function it provides and the financial function its backers believe it will eventually produce. Social shaping, from culture to technology and back again, will continue, as evidenced by Sheryl Sandberg's (chief operating officer of Facebook) prediction for the future of the social network:

Expressing our authentic identity will become even more pervasive . . . Profiles will no longer be outlines, but detailed self-portraits of who we really are, including the books we read, the music we listen to, the distances we run, the places we travel, the causes we support, the videos of cats we laugh at, our likes and our links . . . this shift will take getting used to and will elicit cries about lost privacy. But people will increasingly recognise the benefits of such expression. Because the strength of social media is that it empowers individuals to amplify and broadcast their voices. The truer that voice, the louder it will sound and the farther it will reach. (quoted in *The Economist*, 2011)

Sandberg's choice of the words "authentic identity" is an interesting one. While this phrase lacks the nuance of the complex nature we know identities hold (discussed in more detail in Chapter Six), it does belie what I believe to be the assumption behind the creation of Facebook, which is that people will use it to "be themselves". While I have been arguing throughout this text (as psychoanalysts have been for more than a century) that "being an authentic self" is itself a complex task and perhaps one that is impossible to fully achieve, much research (Back et al., 2011; Lampe, Ellison, & Steinfield, 2006) does tend to show that users do engage with Facebook in ways that are not enormously different from how they present themselves in the real world. However, as Facebook expands its ecosystem, it becomes more than a forum of self-expression through words on a status update or photos uploaded from last weekend's party; it becomes a presentation of self based on the music one listens to, the newspapers one reads, and a whole variety of other activities that become public through these social applications. The overall effects of this social influence on individuals are immense. As Thaler and Sunstein (2008) suggest, the two basic categories of social influence are *information*—"If many people do something or think something, their actions and their thoughts convey information about what might be best for you to do or think" (p. 54)—and *peer pressure*—"If you care about what other people think of you . . . then you might go along with the crowd to avoid their wrath or curry their favor" (p. 54). Given that Facebook accomplishes both information dispersion and peer pressure with aplomb, the intensity of commercial interest is clearly evident, and its exploitation of its users has consequences for one's internal object relations. Whereas we have already learned that Digital Natives are less likely to differentiate online and offline identities than Digital Immigrants (Palfrey & Gasser, 2008), this is likely to change over the next decade with the increased probability of the blurring of identities right across the demographic spectrum (Foresight Future Identities, 2013).

The challenge of the blurring and differentiation of identities is increasing on several levels because aspects of an individual's identity that are based on that person's tastes and consumption habits are now being conflated with *representations* of themselves across networked publics that are enabled by online convenience and the ease of public disclosure. No doubt similar issues to these were present long before the advent of online social networking; however, the perpetual existence of ourselves in virtual space alongside the growing commercial eco-system that colonises more and more aspects of our lives amplifies these consequences.

Narcissism is about people, not social networks

While the commercial pressures within the growing architecture of Facebook risks objectifying the subject who uses it, there are more fundamental psychodynamics going on that function like hooks upon which these commercial motivations are hung. These dynamics take us back to the need for recognition and the ways in which agencies of the ego, such as the false self and the persona, step up to consume partial recognition across SNSs. The dominant feature in cultural criticism and social anxiety in relation to Facebook and other SNSs is that they breed narcissism and that for this reason they are deleterious to meaningful social ties. The link between narcissism and the nature of relationships lies in the narcissistic dynamic of making other subjects into objects in the mind of the narcissist: as if they were extensions of the self. Narcissism is a tricky concept that is understood in a variety of ways across the psychological disciplines. It has different meanings even within the varying schools of psychoanalysis, let alone in experimental psychology, where it is closely associated with personality profiling and psychometrics. Narcissism has a long and complex history in psychoanalysis, dating back to Freud. Laplanche and Pontalis (1988) detail its meaning in psychoanalysis by directing us to the myth of Narcissus before summarising pithily that narcissism is, "love directed towards the image of oneself" (p. 255); this is followed by a more comprehensive tracking of the theory through Freud's work.[24] McLuhan (1964), reflecting on the same myth, notes the etymological relationship between the name *Narcissus*, and the Greek word *narcosis*, or numbness:

> The youth Narcissus mistook his own reflection in the water for another person. This extension of himself by mirror numbed his perceptions until he became the servomechanism of his own extended or repeated image ... Obviously he would have had very different feelings about the image had he known it was an extension or repetition of himself ... It is, perhaps, indicative of the bias of our intensely technological and therefore narcotic culture that we have long interpreted the Narcissus story to mean that he fell in love with himself, that he imagined the reflection to be Narcissus. (pp. 45–46)

McLuhan's reading is rich with meaning in relation to technology in his day as much as it is in ours. First, McLuhan reminds us that Narcissus did not *know* that he was merely falling in love with an *image* of himself. Today, the general cultural sense of narcissism misses this crucial point, taking a rather punitive perspective on "self love" as a rather simplistic version of ego inflation, resulting in the holding up of the narcissistic individual as a subject of derision. Narcissus, rather, is *lost* in his own reflection; the love for himself is not a direct self-love as it is not directed at the actual true self. Rather, it is a lost and disembodied feeling for which "love" is really a misnomer. Narcissus is extended outside himself, reflected back and repeated again and again, producing qualities of self-love that have a numbing *anti*-relational effect. In relation to Benjamin's (1988) mutual recognition, we can see that there can be no mutuality in the reflected image of narcissistic loving because the "love" is just that, reflected back rather than being filtered through the lens of the "other", which is a wholly different subjectivity. The whole point of mutual recognition is that the love is reflected back through a different subjectivity; the depth of intersubjectivity is lodged in this space of difference. Narcissism lacks this depth because it lacks a fundamental sense of the other as *real*. What the narcissist receives, then, is not self-love at all, but a compensatory and vulnerable preoccupation with a reflection of the false self.

In the broadest sense, narcissism operates on a continuum from what can be regarded as non-pathological narcissism, demonstrated in a healthy self-regard and confidence, to a pathological condition of the personality itself, that which the *DSM-IV-TR* classifies as a narcissistic personality disorder (NPD), which is described as "A pervasive pattern of grandiosity (in fantasy or behavior), need for admiration, and lack of empathy, beginning in early adulthood and present in a variety of contexts" (American Psychiatric Association, 2000, p. 717). Some of the criteria that would invite a diagnoses of NPD are: feelings of being special; a sense of entitlement; lacking in empathy and exploiting others; envy and arrogance (p. 717). Narcissism must be understood within the context of our wider culture, particularly in the West, which has been seen by many cultural theorists as a narcissistic culture in its own right (Lasch, 1979). Johnson (1987) subscribes to the force of cultural influence on narcissism in his rather compassionate approach to what he calls a "narcissistic style" that was induced by both culture and familial constellations:

> [The narcissistic style is] part and parcel of our life-denying culture, which places accomplishment over pleasure, status over love,

appearance over reality. It is the endemic result of our culture's material perfectionism. It bridles a very significant proportion of people
and cripples some of our most gifted and giving individuals. Yet while
the culture reinforces it, its breeding ground is the family. (p. 3)

The way in which online social networking can enable the narcissistic style is a component of online culture, rather than a new technological production of narcissism itself. For Johnson, the narcissistic
adult is doing her best to cope with having been a "used child" in
which the dominant message from primary care-givers was "Don't be
who you are, be who I need you to be. Who you are disappoints me,
threatens me, angers me, overstimulates me. Be what I want and I will
love you" (Johnson, 1987, p. 39). A hallmark of any psychodynamic
approach is the importance it places on early family relationships and
their capacity to lay down relational templates that become repeated
throughout life. For Johnson (1994), a narcissistic style often develops
in relation to the damage inflicted upon the real self, damage which
ultimately invites a narcissistic response to narcissistic injury:

> The injury is a deep wound to the experience of the real self. In the
> more extreme cases . . . the person has no residual experience or
> comprehension of the real self. In the less extreme variations . . . *which
> are endemic to the culture*, there is often a veiled awareness of the real
> self but a concomitant rejection of it. (p. 155, my italics)

Ronningstam (2005) also notes the cultural aspect of narcissism as
a particularly Western phenomena:

> Comparisons between the individualistically, 'I'-oriented Western
> cultures and the collectivistic 'we'-oriented Eastern cultures have indi-
> cated that Western cultures, which promote inner separateness and
> independent self-motivation, assertiveness, and mobility, would urge
> narcissistic functioning and lay the foundation for the development of
> narcissistic personality disorder. (p. 43)

Ronningstam goes on to describe the cultural embeddedness of NPD
by noting its controversial absence from the World Health Organization's equivalent of the American *DSM*, the *ICD-10*.[25] Such is the international reach of the *DSM*, however, that its diagnostic categories are
being co-opted around the word by other countries in any case. This
phenomenon is interestingly echoed in the development of SNSs, too.

The most popular ones, such as Faceboook and Twitter, have been developed in the USA and are colonising the rest of the world. Facebook, for example, has either taken over or is fast approaching being the top-used SNS in countries such as India and Brazil, where other SNSs had previously been preferred (Swift, 2012). Where Western (particularly American) diagnostic categories were once exported across the world, now its social networks are doing the same. Are they exporting with them a particular Western narcissistic style as well?

In distinct relational terms, narcissism, in the simplest sense, is a defence produced in response to misrecognition (when recognition fails and the parent sees the child as an object, or as an extension of the parent's own self) and the child responds by amplifying an attachment to their own ego, which becomes invested in the false self. The false self, in this instance, is the part responding to the command (implicit or explicit) of "being who I am needed to be" (false self) rather than being "who I am, reflected in my mother's eyes" (true self); the direction in which an individual leans in their narcissistic styling is likely to indicate how they manage their online selves when social networking. The way in which online social networking lends itself to the presentation of self encourages not narcissism, *per se*, but, rather, a presented self that looks for reflection from others (imagined audiences, networked publics), reflections that can be experienced as a "fix" for the narcissistic needs in all of us.

Facebook enables recognition through functions such as its "like" button, which allows others to mark appreciation of a user's content. A status update, photo, or witty comment will attract "likes" and further comments that operate as strokes to the user's ego. The term "strokes" comes from the tradition of transactional analysis and is defined by Berne (1964) as "any act implying recognition of another's presence . . . the fundamental unit of social action. An exchange of strokes constitutes a *transaction* which is a unit of social intercourse" (p. 15). On Twitter, one finds a similar phenomenon to the trading of strokes. A tweet can be re-tweeted, favourited, or it may attract new followers, all actions that signal to the user that the tweet was good, appreciated, *recognised* as worthy; each response to a tweet gives the ego a positive stroke. By way of unconscious operant conditioning, tweets can become engineered to attract such strokes. Alternatively, both platforms can also make a user vulnerable. A Facebook status may be left unliked or a tweet may dissolve into the ether unresponded to. Over time, the user learns to gauge his updates, posts, or tweets to increase engagement. It is likely that the presentation of self is seeking a kind of recognition that is accumulated via the false self, or persona, producing a dynamic that can enable narcissistic engagement. However, the way in which an individual may engage narcissistically with the SNS platform is likely to be in relation to their narcissistic style, which will have been laid down long before they first access an SNS. While a narcissistic engagement is far more likely to emanate from the way in which a user consumes the responses across their network than anything essential about the SNS itself, online networks are, no doubt, amenable to narcissistic engagement in the same way that they are tilted towards false-self expression. This style is related to false-self development and empathic failure in the facilitating environment. This is precisely where psychoanalyst Heinz Kohut locates narcissism: in the failure of the empathic parental response. "Kohut strongly states that the essential part of mothering consists of empathic attention and caring towards the infant *as if there were already a self*" (Curk, 2007, p. 75). Part and parcel of the empathic mothering response is the act of mirroring, the way in which the primary care-taker mirrors back the unique subjectivity of the child. Mirroring, by all accounts, is about reflection; however, Benjamin (1988) points out that reflection alone is not enough:

> The mother cannot (and should not) be a mirror; she must not merely reflect back what the child asserts; she must embody something of the not-me; she must be an independent other who responds in her different way. Indeed, as the child increasingly establishes his own independent centre of existence, her recognition will be meaningful only to the extent that it reflects her own equally separate subjectivity. (p. 24)

In a later work, Benjamin (1998) makes a corollary to the analytic situation in which the analyst is stripped of objectivity about the patient's experience, rather

> we acknowledge the analyst's participation in an interaction of two subjects. The double action of intersubjectivity – recognizing the other's subjectivity and one's own – means that as the patient becomes less objectified, the analyst becomes a more 'subjective' object. (p. 24)

A further corollary can be drawn to the online social networking environment, in which the seeking of mirroring and pure reflection would be indicative of a narcissistic aim of the user while a more open and impactful dialogue would be indicative of a mutual intersubjectivity. The architecture of the social network offers both of these possibilities through the assumed presence of being engaged in a networked public with imagined audiences, a set-up that has particular consequences for the nature of an individual's engagement. In sum, each of the psychodynamic models referenced above point to developmental deficits in the early family environment that can provoke narcissistic styling as a defensive response: this styling can then be deployed across the online social network.

Much of the press and social commentary that concerns itself with narcissism and social networking, however, is not anchored in these psychodynamic traditions as much as it is informed by the field of experimental psychology. As a rule, experimental psychology is less interested in developmental psychodynamics (personal narratives, symbolisation, unconscious process, etc.) and concentrates more on identifying the nature of narcissism as it exists in groups and individuals, primarily as one of the "big five" personality traits that we all share to varying degrees. In experimental psychology, these elements of narcissism are, none the less, closely related to descriptions from psychodynamic theory. Buffardi and Campbell (2008) describe narcissism thus:

> Narcissism refers to a personality trait reflecting a grandiose and inflated self-concept . . . Narcissists do not focus on interpersonal intimacy, warmth, or to the positive long-term relational outcomes, but they are very skilled at both initiating relationships and using relationships to look popular, successful, and high in status in the short term. (p. 1304)

In academic and experimental psychology, narcissism is tested using the Narcissistic Personality Inventory (NPI) which is a multiple-choice questionnaire given to "non-clinical" individuals to answer via self-report. It measures narcissism in terms of leadership/authority, superiority/arrogance, self-absorption/self-admiration, and vulnerability/sensitivity (Ronningstam, 2005, p. 28). Nearly all of the research I have encountered that looks at narcissism and social networking operates from the academic psychological approach, and most have utilised the NPI. Buffardi and Campbell (2008), for example, used the

NPI in their research of university undergraduates to see whether narcissism was manifested across an SNS (in this case, Facebook). They postulate that SNSs may be:

> an especially fertile ground for narcissists to self-regulate via social connections for two reasons. First, narcissists function well in the context of shallow (as opposed to emotionally deep and committed) relationships. Social networking Web [*sic*] sites are built on the base of superficial 'friendships' with many individuals and 'sound-byte' driven communication between friends (e.g. *wallposts*). Certainly, individuals use social networking sites to maintain deeper relationships as well, but often the real draw is the ability to maintain large numbers of relationships (e.g. many users have many hundreds or even thousands of 'friends'). Second, social networking Web pages are highly controlled environments. (p. 1304)

The bias in this research is clear in the disparaging tone it takes towards "narcissists", who are seen to be a category of person that appears to lack any complexity or depth (cf. Johnson's (1987, 1994) more compassionate approach), as well as the judgement that SNSs are "built on the base of superficial friendships". Contrastingly, as will be discussed in the following chapter, online social networks such as Facebook are not only fundamentally built upon existing "real" relationships (Hampton, Goulet, Rainie, & Purcell, 2011), but users do distinguish between different kinds of relationships across Facebook, that is, if a user has a great many Facebook friends, their closer friends will be maintained differently than their acquaintances (Marlow, 2009). Perhaps Buffardi and Campell's perspective has something to do with the date of their research (2008), which, in online social networking terms, occurred some time ago. None the less, the sense that SNSs are essentially shallow and narcissistic continues, despite Buffardi and Campbell's unremarkable conclusion "that narcissists act, portray themselves, and are perceived on social networking sites in a manner similar to how they behave in real offline life" (p. 1312): this finding is hardly alarming. Furthermore, the researchers admit a caveat in their research in that their subjects were all of a similar age (undergraduates, the great fodder of psychological testing), and second, that the estimations of narcissism were acquired from anonymous judges, not by people in their own social network (as would be the case on Facebook outside the confines of a psychological study).

Additionally, in correlating activity on Facebook (such as posting photos, or "self-promoting") the authors admit, "Although the sizes of these effects are small, given the complexity and the nuances of Facebook profiles, they are notable" (p. 1310). Frequently, it is just these sorts of tenuous conclusions that are ultimately inflated in the press stories that follow them. While it remains clear that online social networking sites can be a platform on which a narcissist can thrive, they probably do so more or less as they would across other social platforms.

Narcissism as a social projection of anxiety

Buffardi and Campell's research came to the rather banal conclusion that if one has a narcissistic disposition before engaging on an SNS, then they are likely to behave narcissistically *on* an SNS. Similarly, Ryan and Xenos's (2011) study came to an equally mundane conclusion, stating that "The data relating to more specific Facebook usage confirms [that] Facebook gratifies its users in different ways depending on their individual characteristics" (p. 1663). In a wide-ranging systematic review, Nadkarni and Hofmann (2012) came up with several findings that also seem to correlate behaviour on Facebook with the expression of a personality style across the platform, including the fact that extraverts tend to use Facebook more, shy individuals had fewer Facebook friends than non-shy individuals, and that both individuals with high narcissism and those with low self esteem spent more than an hour a day on the network. They, rather confusingly, conclude that

> the review of the literature of FB use suggests that a high level of extra-version, low self esteem, high levels of neuroticism, narcissism, and low levels of self esteem and self-worth are associated with high FB use. Frequent FB use is also associated with lower academic performance but possibly higher self esteem and sense of belonging (Nadkarni & Hofmann, 2012, p. 245)

I believe that the reason for this garbled conclusion is that Nadkarni and Hofmann's systematic review was looking at forty-two "evidence based" studies that took a nomothetic approach to understanding the reasons why people used Facebook. While such studies are important to get an understanding of some generalities, most are large-scale and dependent on psychological instruments such as psychometric measures that do not provide in-depth information about individual motivations, how individuals understand their Facebook use, or the meaning that users make out of their online relational experiences. Furthermore, while some of this research provides information that is "statistically significant" it is another question as to whether it is meaningful or not. For example, in Ryan and Xenos's (2011) study, a correlation was found between exhibitionism and a preference for status updates. However, the r value (a measure of correlation) was a tiny 0.06 (1 is a perfect positive correlation and -1 is a perfect negative correlation). While the p value of 0.039 indicated that the correlation was very unlikely to have occurred by chance, making it "statistically significant", it is still a very small relationship between the two, calling the *meaningfulness* of the findings into question.

Reporting on social networking research in the media, however, rarely honestly tells the story of the research itself, throwing another layer of misapprehension into the public sphere. By tracking the story of just one headline I encountered in my research for this book, we can see how fear and hysteria about social networking are spread even though they are completely de-coupled from the research itself. In August of 2011, Emma Barnett, the digital media editor at the *Telegraph*, published an article under the following headline, "Social network overuse 'breeds Narcissism'". This rather hyperbolic headline was based on a paper, given in August of 2011 by Larry Rosen at the American Psychological Association's annual conference, entitled "Poke me: how social networking can both help and harm our kids" (Rosen, 2011). While Rosen's paper took a balanced approach to the negative and positive aspects of online social networking (as clearly represented in its title), Barnett's article (among many others) picked up much more on the negative ways in which SNSs can be blamed for a number of young people's ills, including the encouragement of "vain, aggressive and anti-social behaviour . . . bouts of anxiety, depression and other psychological disorders" and lower academic achievement (Barnett, 2011). The article does admit, at the end, that social networks do have some positive effects as well, including helping shy young people socialise and, contrastingly, improving academic performance through interactive learning. However, the overall tone of the article, as led by its headline, is clearly negative. In following up this article, I found that Barnett's piece in the *Telegraph* was just one of scores of hyperbolic headlines that arose from Rosen's talk, including "Psychologist: Facebook harmful to kids", and "Do social networking sites create anti-social behavior?" (Rosen, 2011). While there were plenty of more balanced headlines, too (e.g., "Facebook makes teens narcissistic, anxious and depressed—but also nice, social, and engaged"), even these were, none the less, misleading (Facebook does not "make" teens any of those things). Rosen himself was so shocked by the media coverage of his speech that he was compelled to write a response in *Psychology Today*. In his response, Rosen shares his shock and concern about how rapidly his talk was disseminated and altered across the press,

> When all was said and done I realized that the fact that my talk title mentioned how social networking could 'help' AND 'harm' children meant nothing to the media . . . overall I would say that maybe 10% of the articles dealt with both sides of the issue but that is to be expected since controversy sells newspapers. (Rosen, 2011)

Rosen then goes on to find another article in the respected journal *Pediatrics*, which states that researchers have proposed "a new phenomenon called 'Facebook Depression'" based on a misquote in which one of the leading researchers was supposed to have said that social networking, texting, and messaging "can lead to depression" an incorrect quote that "created a life of its own" (Rosen, 2011). Social networking researchers, it seems, are vulnerable to having their findings twisted to reflect social myths rather than the facts of the research itself. While the media is notoriously bad at communicating the specifics of scientific research in any discipline (see Goldacre's 2009 work on medicine and public health), the way in which social networking research is reported seems to invite similar and repeated themes, such as can be seen in the sampling of headlines here:

"Social media: an epidemic of narcissism" (Forrester, 2011)

"Facebook's 'dark side': study finds link to socially aggressive narcissism" (Pearse, 2012)

"Social networks and the narcissism epidemic" (Tobak, 2012)

"Is social media to blame for the rise in narcissism?" (Firestone, 2012)

A Google search of "Facebook" and "Narcissism" comes up with 3.5 million hits in a mere 0.41 seconds. If there is a great demon of the social network, it does seem to be narcissism, but this fear is simply not unequivocally borne out in the research. Nadkarni and Hofmann (2012) conclude from their systematic review that, rather than promoting narcissism, Facebook is simply a venue of self-presentation like any other:

> Taken together, these studies [contained with the systematic review] suggest that FB profiles may reflect the users' public persona, which appears to be shaped and motivated by the need for self-presentation. This need appears to guide the users' specific behaviors, such as choice of profile photo and number of friends connections, which are in line with the user's desired impression formation. (p. 247)

It is unlikely that the way an individual might take care to present him or herself at a party or social gathering would invite the charge of "narcissism" unless they showed up in a particular way that invited such a response. People tend to put their best face on in most public environments, and although Facebook has a number of qualities that no doubt affect the ways in which individuals choose to present themselves, in other ways it is quite simply just another public environment. Nadkarni and Hofmann's (2012) research backs up this common sense idea in noting that most people show up on Facebook in similar ways to how they do in their daily lives, put rather simply, ". . . because the *need to belong* and the *need for self-presentation* reflect general personality traits, we assume that similar behavioral patterns are evident in a person's behavior offline, which mirror the behavior online" (pp. 247–248). It is curious that, although the research continues to point to the conclusion that individuals will behave on Facebook no differently than they do in real life, the public fear of rampant narcissism continues unabated. Why might this be so?

My sense is that this fear is legitimate, but that it is misplaced. There is little doubt that while social networking and the general ubiquitous nature of online culture as described in Chapter Three provide a variety of different "connected-up" experiences, the way in which these experiences are offered up tend to be at the easier and wider end of the intersubjective spectrum, rather than at the narrower and deeper end. By this, I mean that it might be easier to maintain certain more casual relationships online than it is to manage relational depth online. Furthermore, the ease of casual online interaction may make it more desirable for some to relate in that paradigm than to engage in the sometimes difficult experience that offline relational depth often requires. Online communication is a largely cognitive phenomenon. Despite the fact that it invites an emotional response, online life can lack a sense of embodiment. Orbach (2009) warns that there can be hazards when there is a lack of embodiment, "[t]he absence of embodiment does strange things to people. It dematerialises their existence . . ." (p. 79). In this sense, the lack of full-bodied awareness that can be experienced in offline intersubjectivity can promote an ungrounded feeling: a relational experience that feels as if it is going on in the head rather than in the heart. Winnicott (1960) similarly warns of what he calls the "intellectual defence" where "there is a very strong tendency for the mind to become the location of the False Self, and in this case there develops a dissociation between intellectual activity and psychosomatic existence" (p. 144). The lean towards a cognitive engagement promotes intellectualisation and body-distant experience, while the ease of interaction invites a lukewarm sort of relating that may be free of the difficulties of the deep intersubjective encounter. In Chapter One, I suggested that online social networking is often seen like the fast food of intersubjective relating. In its "relational-lite", convenient way, online social networking does seem to operate as such much of the time; it feels good, but may not always be nourishing. Turkle (2011) notes now technology may be giving us more of what we think we want than what we need:

> one might assume that what we want is to be always in touch and never alone, no matter who or what we are in touch with. One might assume that what we want is a preponderance of weak ties, the informal networks that underpin online acquaintanceship. But if we pay attention to the real consequences of what we think we want, we may discover what we really want, we may want some stillness and solitude. (pp. 284–285)

While, at bottom, we might want the challenge, difficulty, and rewards of deep and intimate relating, or, alternatively, to enjoy the capacity to be alone, we may in any case reach out for an easy bit of online relating in the same way as we grab a potato crisp; it tastes good, but it will not nourish us. Online social networking gives us a plethora of choice, but, as we have seen, these choices are not neutral;

they are embedded in its architecture. It has both capacities to promote the nourishment of intimate relating or the fix of a fast food relational hit. It is these elements of the virtual world that promotes a sense of the unknown, a sense of fear that is projected on to easy words like narcissism. Narcissism works because it embodies the very nature of being objectified, and becoming an object imperils relational depth.

The nature of online friendships

So, we find that there is a grain of truth in the dangers that online social networking may provoke with regard to the nature of our relationships. However, as we have seen, much of the cultural commentary on the issue is both under-informed, marginally hysterical, and problematically conflates different aspects and components of a highly complex and rich system into unhelpful conclusions about the health or pathology of SNSs as a whole. Greene (2012), outlines a series of popular complaints that are frequently associated with the popularity of Facebook:

> The word 'friend' is being devalued by having hundreds upon hundreds of 'friends'. Users' pages are not a genuine portrait, but a careful selection of photos and updates that amount to an illusion. People should be enjoying their vacation, not taking hundreds of pictures of it and putting them on Facebook. People should spend more time curling up with real books, not waste time bragging about what they read via GoodReads. The birthday messages that pour in because Facebook told your 'Friends' it was your birthday are no substitute for real friends who actually remember. (p. 75)

This is a familiar litany of concerns that continues unabated. The previous chapter introduced us to Carr's (2010) worries about an intellectual "shallowing" that can be induced by the particular mechanics of the Web. While social networking was not really a central focus of his book, none the less, he continues to see the potential for the same shallowing effect across SNSs "[b]y turning intimate messages—once the realm of the letter, the phone call, the whisper—into fodder for a new form of mass media" (p. 158). In this, Carr's concern seems to be the way in which what once seemed "intimate" is now deployed as "fodder" across the social network. Burkeman (2012), writing for the *Guardian*, turns his attention to the relational nature of the SNS "friend" and makes clear his concerns about how SNSs in particular enable the shallowing out of interpersonal relationships, particularly through the networks of Facebook, LinkedIn, and Twitter. Burkeman opines about the various levels of friendships that need to be maintained (as a form of work) across these networks, admitting "with a feeling of dismay . . . I've started to think of some of these contacts – not most of them, but some – as clutter". He goes on to say that "Friend clutter . . . accumulates because it's effortless to accumulate it: before the Internet, the only bonds you'd retain were the ones you actively cultivated . . . or those with a handful of people you saw every day". Burkeman offers up a sense of futility with having to deal with the clutter of friends and contacts, while at the same time he recognises, by saying "not most of them, but some", that a "friend" is not always a *friend*. Despite all the cries to the contrary, as we will explore in the following chapter, people do seem to know the difference between one and the other, spending more time interacting with their "maintained relationships" while more passively keeping up with their acquaintances and more distant relationships through their newsfeeds (Marlow, 2009). Nevertheless, Burkeman's perspective shows us that this blurring of the line between a contact and a friend can create a relational burden in which our friends become a new form of virtual clutter that needs to be occasionally cleaned out. Seeing it this way offers a frightening perspective on how online relationships can feel burdensome, and, hence, shallow and expendable. Clutter, no doubt, is for objects, not subjects.

The nature of social ties, particularly in relation to their depth and/or shallowness is a strong indicator of feelings of loneliness or connection to others. Marche (2012), in an article in *The Atlantic*, tracks the increase in loneliness and isolation in the USA through a series of studies. Although he notes that there is complexity behind the causes of reported loneliness and the reasons are variable and not entirely predictive (whether one is married or has religious faith, etc.), he does track a steady trajectory towards more loneliness that is clearly related to the quality and amount of social interaction. Marche's research provoked him to ask that popular and growing question, "Does the Internet make people lonely, or are lonely people more attracted to the Internet?" As it turns out, it is a matter of degree, as Marche found out when interviewing Facebook researcher Moira Burke about an on-going and as yet unpublished longitudinal study of 1,200 Facebook users. Burke has found, in resonance with what we have already discussed above, that one gets out of Facebook what one puts into it. For example, "one click communication" (e.g., "liking" a status) produced no change in loneliness, while a "composed communication" decreased the sense of loneliness; loneliness is further decreased if that communication is sent semi-publicly, for example, posted on a person's wall (Marche, 2012). What Burke calls "passive communication", which would involve scanning other people's profiles but not participating, increases the sense of loneliness. Like most of the research reviewed above, Burke found that what goes on in the offline life is also reflected in online life, at least on Facebook:

> Burke's research does not support the assertion that Facebook creates loneliness. The people who experience loneliness on Facebook are lonely away from Facebook . . . correlation is not causation . . . The depth of one's social network outside Facebook is what determines the depth of one's social network within Facebook, not the other way around. Using social media doesn't create new social networks; it just transfers established networks from one platform to another. For the most part, Facebook doesn't destroy friendships—but it doesn't create them, either. (Marche, 2012)

The research by Hampton, Goulet, Rainie, and Purcell (2011) backs these findings, "if loneliness is measured by the deficit of social ties, we find no evidence that technology plays a negative role" (p. 24). Furthermore, Hampton, Sessions, Her, and Rainie (2009) not only found that frequent Internet users are as likely to participate in community activities as anyone else (dispelling the myth that they would prefer to be home alone with their computers), but also that those using social media in particular are actually more likely to have a more diverse social network, have friends from different back-grounds, races, and members of other political parties, than those who do not participate in such networks. Like the fear that social network-ing *causes* narcissism, we find once again that the related fear of social networking *causing* loneliness or deconstructing the meaning of friendships is also somewhat unfounded. However, we have to take the fear itself seriously, because it is a manifestation of an underlying social anxiety, and again we find that this underlying anxiety is embedded in the fear of having our unique subjectivities undermined in a way that disables authentic relating between subjects. The further one is removed from apprehending another person's subjectivity, the more likely it is that relational damage can occur by treating the other as "less than" in an environment that, rather than facilitating a rich intersubjectivity, facilitates projection.

Projection and the underlying dynamics of trolling and bullying

The persistent cultural fear of a narcissism epidemic instigated by an online social networking culture, although overblown, makes sense in the context of a new technology that is disproportionately taken up by young people whose parents lack sufficient understanding of it. These parents and other Digital Immigrants, who are disproportionally represented in the press and as cultural commentators, have an uncomfortable sense of the ways in which online social networking has the potential to strip away complex and subtle interpersonal intersubjectivity and replace it with rather superficial representations of individuals as self-presenting objects, resulting in the shallowing of relationships. The presence of anxiety in the face of threats to traditional ideas about human interrelationships is understandable within an online environment where direct interpersonal feedback occurs at one step of remove from offline relating. While both narcissism and the shallowing of relationships introduce challenges to the psychodynamics of intersubjectivity, they neither represent malicious intent nor a direct attack on others. Psychoanalysis has long understood the impediments to direct interpersonal relating, even when it is face to face. The psychoanalytic concepts of transference and projection have long been relational dynamics of interest, both as they appear in the consultation room, where they can be examined closely, and in the outside world, where they are always active but rarely explored. The clinical situation creates conditions in which the dynamics of transference and projection can be unpacked and understood within the therapeutic relationship. Both transference and projection are foundational aspects of the way in which mutual recognition could be inhibited by the ways both patient and analyst apprehend each other.

Transference, for example, occurs when unconscious dynamics from the earliest relationships are re-enacted with the therapist, and the patient responds to the therapist in ways that they would have responded to key individuals in those previous relationships. Laplanche and Pontalis (1988) note that this occurs with a "strong sense of immediacy" (p. 455) which indicates the sense of realness that is often present in transference situations. In other words, when one is in the grip of a transference, it feels very much like the "real relationship", even when the core of the current transferential enactment might be based upon projections of earlier relational patterning. Although transference is not generally considered a defence, it is an aspect of relating that can obscure the clarity of truly seeing the other that is so essential in mutual recognition. The more one is obscured, the more easily one can fall into a transference, making SNSs amenable to high levels of transference. Projection is intimately related to transference, although it is considered a defence in which "qualities, feelings, wishes or even 'objects', which the subject refuses to recognise or rejects in himself, are expelled from the self and located in another person or thing" (Laplanche & Pontalis, 1988, p. 349). Like transference, projection has the same strong sense of immediacy, and when it is activated it feels as if it is part of the "real relationship". Both transference and projection are related to what Winnicott (1986) referred to as the subjective perceiving of the object (to be explored further in the following chapter) in which the other is not perceived as a subject in their own right, but through the lens of the self, ultimately altering the way in which the other is perceived. The more the other is perceived as an object instead of a subject, the more the dynamics of transference and projection will come to fill in the gaps. While transference occurs all the time in ways that are both subtle and complex, projection, when operated as a primitive defence against internal anxieties, can be deployed in ways that are hurtful to the other; the most pernicious form of projection that occurs online results in cyberbullying and trolling.

Smith and colleagues (2008) define cyberbullying as "An aggressive, intentional act carried out by a group or individual, *using electronic forms of contact*, repeatedly and over time against a victim who cannot easily defend him or herself" (p. 376, original italics). This definition was created by adding the italicised words to a definition of what has come to be known as "traditional" bullying, defined by Olweus (1993). Like the fear of narcissism, the fear of cyberbullying is likely to be somewhat overblown. Although incidences of it are no doubt hurtful and a certain cause for concern and intervention, research carried out by Görzig (2011) reports that online bullying might not be as rampant as is reported in the press. According to Görzig, only six per cent of nine- to sixteen-year-olds report having been bullied online with only half that number admitting to doing the bullying; similarly to live bullying, those who have been bullied tend to be children who were already vulnerable (Görzig, 2011). Smith and colleagues' (2008) research suggests that cyberbullying may be under-reported because it tends to happen outside of schools; however, their study also supports the notion that cyberbullying operates in ways that are not so different from traditional bullying. Their research showed that those who were victimised by traditional bullies were likely to be victims of cyberbullies and that those who acted as traditional bullies were more likely to be cyberbullies. However, as cyberbullying was reported as less frequent than traditional bullying, many traditional bullies and victims did not have cyber-equivalent experiences (Smith et al. 2008, p. 381). O'Keefe and Clark-Pearson (2011), while also concurring that online harassment is not as common as offline harassment, still importantly maintain that "cyberbullying is quite common, can occur to any young person online, and can cause profound psychosocial outcomes including depression, anxiety, severe isolation, and tragically, suicide" (p. 810). These consequences are much the same as with traditional bullying, although one of the main differences lies in the fact that in cyberbullying, an individual may be bullied while by themselves at home or at any other time or place by way of their mobile phone.

In Chapter Two, we discussed how the nature of virtual impingement operates in relation to an individual when they are on their own and in a particularly vulnerable state. With cyberbullying, this impingement is purposeful, which naturally has further consequences. However, in relation to how cyberbullying is deployed, research by Smith and colleagues (2008) found, through focus groups, that being anonymously bullied could operate either as a protective factor or it could induce greater fear because the victim did not know where the attack was coming from. Similarly, cyberbullying could be worse because the victim might be alone when experiencing it, or, alternatively, could feel safer because there was proof of the event that could be shared with others (Smith et al., 2008, p. 381). Clearly, the damage inflicted depends on a variety of over-determined factors based on the context of the situation and the individuals involved. Further, Smith and colleagues' findings support the notion that the distancing and objectifying effect of online life that enables projection is an important factor in cyberbullying. In focus groups with secondary school students, Smith's team found that:

> Some perceived the bully's motivation as due to a lack of confidence and desire for control: 'bullying on the computer is quite cowardly, because they can't face up to the person themselves; people are too scared to do stuff face to face'; 'there is less fear of getting caught'. Another theme was how the lack of face-to-face interaction in cyberbullying reduces empathy in bullies. Cyberbullying was often described as entertainment: they do it more for fun; 'they just get bored and were entertaining themselves'. (p. 380)

The interpersonal distance that Internet relating provides offers individuals a particular kind of environment that might facilitate projection and attack by reducing direct consequential feedback. Anonymity increases the prevalence and veracity of the attack by increasing the distance between the bully and the object of the bullying. boyd (2008), in her research on young people and social networks, noted that the teens she interviewed "conceded that technology could amplify bullying, but they did not believe that technology was the root cause of it" (p. 245); the real danger lay in the "ability to copy and paste conversations and access interactions asynchronously [which] can amplify the spread of gossip and magnify the cost of bullying" (p. 251). Wolak, Mitchell, and Finklehor (2007) suggest that a distinction is made between cyberbullying and online harassment, noting that bullying is often seen to occur in the school environment (or an extension of that) while harassment is much wider.

Trolling is a kind of harassment that is generally expressed in online public forums with the primary intent of provoking readers into an emotional response. Trolling does not occur frequently in online social networks of known others (like Facebook) because it relies on anonymity, which most SNSs lack. Trolling occurs in other non-SNS social environments, such as chat rooms, blogs, and comment pages, and often disturbingly shows the extremities of behaviour that projection can bring to bear when deployed by way of modern social technologies. Lanier (2011) notes that in most online social environments (such as websites with comment pages to which comments can be delivered anonymously), trolling is "the status quo in the online world" (p. 61). Refreshingly, Lanier accepts the troll in himself, and gives us some psychoanalytic insight as to its potential source:

> I notice that I can suddenly become relieved when someone else in an online exchange is getting pounded or humiliated, because that means I'm safe for the moment . . . But that also means I'm complicit in a mob dynamic. (p. 60)

The result that Lanier describes is the very nature of projection in a group environment in which the bad objects are all projected on to the same source (the scapegoat) providing a sense of relief to others in the group. He also relates to the dynamics of object-to-object relating when he states, "If the troll is anonymous and the target is known then the dynamic is even worse than an encounter between anonymous fragmentary pseudo-people. That's when the hive turns against personhood" (p. 60). While anonymity, as shown above, can be a protective factor against harassment, being the object of a crowd's projections can be distressing. This was demonstrated in January 2013 when, after Professor Mary Beard appeared in the BBC programme *Question Time*, she was brutally trolled in a particular online forum in ways that far exceeded rational responses to the opinions she expressed in the show. The *Observer* reported, "The level of abuse was so shocking that even those accustomed to the cut-and-thrust of online debate were appalled" (Day, 2013, p. 31). When Beard became aware of the abuse, she felt a "sense of assault" at the degree of the vitriol. She understood from her experience that

> there's real frustration coming out in those vile comments. Sure, it's misogyny, but it is also alienation and resentment, understandably, about the voice and the right to speak. The web is democratising and also the voice of people who don't think they have another outlet. And that voice can be punitive. (Day, 2013, p. 31)

Like Lanier, Beard is putting her finger on the nature of projection here, and what it feels like to be the object of that projection; in this case the projection was within an online group dynamic deploying projection as an externalisation of conflict (Hinshelwood, 1991, p. 398). After some time, Beard understood that she was being used as an object of projection, understanding this process served as a protective factor, "It was so ghastly it didn't feel personal, or personally critical . . . It was such generic violent misogyny. In a way, I didn't feel it was about me" (Day, 2013). While Beard was not directly using a psychoanalytic methodology to understand what happened (as far as I know), the dynamics she came to understand fall into the psychoanalytic paradigm with a relatively good fit. Her relief in coming to understand that she was part of a larger group psychodynamic process clearly indicates *how a psychodynamic approach may not only be used to understand these processes, but to helpfully attend to them as well.* This most recent example serves again to illustrate the complex mix that online social environments offer. As we extend ourselves into its matrix, we might become objects for others' projections, our selves become accessible in the perpetual online nature of social environments. These events, whether it is Beard's being under attack, the cultural fear of the loss of the traditional idea of friendship, the shallowing of our intimate relationships relationship, or the growth of narcissism, are all representative of our fears of objectification.

The domain of the social network is an enormous one, vast and still rather new, so it is little wonder that it provokes such strong feelings as we stand by and witness its development in our own lives and the lives of the younger generation, which knows nothing different. It is no wonder it causes anxieties. While many of these anxieties, as they are expressed in the media and by cultural commentators, might be in some ways cut off from what is actually found to be going on across online social networks, the anxieties themselves are important indicators. From the psychoanalytic perspective, they can be seen as symptoms. When an individual has symptoms, the analyst tries to understand the meaning of those symptoms, and, by understanding that meaning, and working it through, the individual patient finds relief. Here, we seek to find the social meaning of the symptom of those anxieties related to social networking that, no doubt, are founded in at least a grain of truth. This truth, I believe, is related to the potential of a great loss, and that great loss is the way in which we as human beings need to be maintained positively in the minds of others. Online social networking can be seen as a stand-in, a threat to authentic relating in which, at an unconscious level, we fear that our identities will somehow be lost. After all, remaining in the mind of another is a foundational need, as we find ourselves in that other's gaze. Narcissism, that great fear, arises when there is not an adequate gaze given back, therefore the gaze is turned inward and we try, failingly, to do that job for ourselves. Both remaining in the mind of another and allowing the other, in their full subjectivity, to remain in the mind of the self offers a solution towards softening a narcissistic style, creating the very conditions that would address it. However, being in the mind of the other, and vice versa, also invites its own anxieties.

CHAPTER FIVE

Being in the mind of the other

"The way people interact reveals implied or tacit assumptions about their relation to the self as object. Each person forms his own 'culture' through the selection of friends, partners and colleagues. The totality of this object-relational field constitutes a type of holding environment and reveals important assumptions about the person's relation to the self as an object at the more existential level of self management"

(Bollas, 1987, pp. 48–49)

In the previous chapter, we looked into the variety of ways in which an individual may be vulnerable to objectification over an online social network. This gravitational pull towards objectification is somewhat paradoxical, since it fundamentally lies over the innate motivation to be recognised as a full subject, and, subsequently, to recognise the other as such. However, as we have seen, there are aspects embedded within the architecture of online social networking that might work in a synergistic way with the functions of false self and persona, transference and projection, that encourage relating as an object to objects rather than the fuller form of intersubjective relating. The dynamics of internal object relations as they are experienced within the subject as well as projected outwards are always in play with *an other* in the relational matrix, both on and offline. However, unlike with online relating, interpersonal cues in offline relationships provide a context in which a lean towards intersubjectivity is encouraged. My own experience, as described in Chapter Two, provides an example of how the intersubjective experience within the consultation room was threatened by the virtual impingement that happened outside that space because it lacked a psychoanalytic "third". A similar concept to the "third" is Winnicott's theory of "holding", that is, both the physical and the loving relationship that creates the relational environment around the infant and its primary care-taker in which the infant is also psychologically *held in mind* by the mother figure. The developmental opportunity that holding offers the infant also includes the growth of the infant's ability to "hold" the image of the mother figure in its own mind (and know that it is also in the mind of the other), which allows the process of separation and individuation to begin. The fundamental process that occurs here is intersubjective. The infant learns that *it is in the mind of the other*, that it is held there, and, thereby, can also internalise the other and keep her inside as an internal companion, enabling the infant to go out and explore the world. The nature of how this process proceeds will go on to inform the quality of its future relationships.

There is a corollary in the online environment that also offers a kind of holding space in which an individual's object and interpersonal relations are activated and challenged. In many ways, as we have discussed above, the online environment operates as an extension of the self where aspects of the self are put online and then responded to by others. These objects (whether they be aspects of the ego, false self, persona, etc.) are seeking something: recognition. As the self is multiply constructed by these objects, it is likely that the recognition needs of each object or self-state may be different; in other words, a single individual may be motivated to seek various forms of recognition, some of which may be at odds with others. By going into an online social environment, the individual is seeking to be in the mind of the other, although, in this case, the other is also multiple, both in terms of their own object relational worlds and of all the possible other individuals within the total online environment. Hence, the self extends into a virtual space that is somewhat unknowable, multiply constructed, and outside of an individual's control, making such an environment liable to invite mechanisms of the ego to seek control. The unconscious dialogue here might be something like: How do I remain in the mind of the other(s) in a way that feels safe and gratifying to me? How is the other represented online to me and what sense do I make of how they reside in *my* mind? How can I control how I can best show up online (and thereby in the mind of the other[s])?

boyd's (2007) "imagined audiences" fulfil an important role here in how the individual presents herself to her viewers, but these audiences are not just imagined, and neither are they simply just *real*, they are, in fact, situated within the minds of others before they are mediated by the online social network. Hartman (2011), reflecting on Winnicott's idea that one of the main human tasks is to keep inner and outer reality separate but interrelated, notes that in the infant's movement from seeing the other as mainly an extension of himself to being able to perceive the other as a subject in her own right, "the baby, given a facilitating environment, comes to recognise that the object inhabits an independent reality external to his omnipotent control" (p. 472). This process results in the developing subject's ability to view the object as external from himself, resulting in a loss of omnipotence and a narrowing of the zone of the self; it also results in the pleasure of discovering another's subjectivity. A similar process can be understood to be occurring when an individual is alone in front of a computer screen; in this online facilitating environment there is more room for the subject to experience a fantasy of omnipotent control simply because the interpersonal feedback is a step removed from what would be experienced in fact-to-face relating. However, in reality, the subject is *less omnipotent than ever before* because her presence online happens instantaneously and is witnessed by many at the very second it occurs. The price for this fantasy of omnipotence is that it inevitably meets with the limits that exist outside of the self (the reality principle), a meeting that can result in anxiety and narcissistic wounding. In this perspective, the online social network is a holding environment in which the degree of being "held" is variable, both in terms of the amount of trust an individual may have about what can be held (based on their own internal object relations) and the fact that they are being held (or not) by multiple witnesses, each with his or her own object relational style and capacity to hold and be held. While the same process holds true for real-life off-line interacting, the additional one step of remove from face-to-face relating alongside the complex mix of the online instantaneous world, where everybody out there is seeking to be in the mind of the other, offers its own unique challenges and opportunities; these challenges occur in a paradoxical environment where both proximity and distance work hand in hand inside the unique matrix of online transitional space.

The paradox of proximity and distance

Proximity and distance are fundamentally related to the way in which we experience relatedness, in both the online and offline life. We often communicate that we feel close to someone or that someone appears "distant". The quality of interpersonal relationships is founded on the principles of proximity and distance and these principles are not necessarily aligned with geographical location. For example, one individual may feel distant from their partner lying next to them in bed, while feeling very close to another individual who is physically quite far away. An SNS such as Facebook, for example, offers a paradoxical situation with regard to the nature of our relating by creating a proximity to some relationships by facilitating closer contact with members of our social networks that may normally have been more distant (such as old high-school friends, acquaintances, or those that live a great distances) while at the same time potentially creating a kind of distance towards other relationships which previously would have been subject to more intimate contact (for example, posting a happy birthday message on a friend's Facebook wall when previously one may have made the effort of putting one in the post). For certain kinds of relationships, an SNS such as Facebook may offer "good enough" contact, perhaps, or even "better than it had been previously", as with friends from long ago with whom, before online social networking, there might have been no contact at all. For other contacts, perhaps those that are closer in an offline capacity, online social networking can have a distancing effect, the ease of the connection preventing a deeper yet more complex and difficult engagement. The architecture of each SNS will have an impact on how proximity and distance are activated psychologically.

The principles of proximity and distance operate quite differently on Twitter, for example, than they do on Facebook. In addition to enabling access to global strangers with shared interests, Twitter provides a democratising and levelling effect that enables easy accessibility to certain individuals such as celebrities, politicians, and admired others, thereby delivering a sense of proximity where there was once distance; this has become a double edged sword, enabling both positive connection and accessibility to attack (via trolling for example) at the same time. While Twitter is by no means only used to follow individuals of notoriety, its democratising effect with regard to celebrity is salient here. Before the social networking revolution, such individuals occupied an idealised space that was felt to be a great distance to most, although they have come much nearer by way of our Twitter feeds. At the celebrity end of the spectrum, Twitter is used primarily as a tool to market one's personality (as an object) rather than as a traditional social network used to connect horizontally to others; this is a dynamic that, in its extremity, puts in relief the objectifying self-promotional activity that is going on with non-celebrities across any online social network, the difference being that, for a celebrity, persona management is a full time job. Nevertheless, these celebrities appear online as relatively levelled, enabling anyone to follow them or watch them converse with each other. High-profile individuals are as vulnerable as anyone else to the slippages that an instantaneous network offers, with many ending up in the spotlight for an opinion inadvisably tweeted (in instance of an expression of another self state slipping by the watchful eyes of the persona: a virtual Freudian slip). The same rules of engagement with regard to the persistence of data apply to them as they do to the rest of us, guaranteeing that their slip will be repeated and shared long after the original tweet was deleted. However the operations and dynamics of proximity and distance are activated by a given network, the very fact that these dynamics occur in virtual space that is in one sense at a distance (experienced as "out there") while at the same time uniquely personal (experienced "in here" between an individual and their computer screen in a "private" space) creates a particular kind of "holding" that is both present and distant, real and unreal, interpersonal and intrapsychic, producing an uncanny replication of the holding environment and all its transitional phenomena.

Virtual space is transitional space

Throughout this text, we have been returning to the earliest moments of psychological development in which formative relationships take place. From the psychodynamic perspective, these early experiences remain central to the psyche as relational templates and are continually returned to in order to understand how they play themselves out, again and again, in contemporary relationships; these experiences are foundational to our subjectivity and fundamental to the ways in which we experience ourselves with others. Online social networking, too, is fundamentally about the way in which we experience ourselves with others, and, for these reasons, they can unconsciously open a re-experiencing of holding within the early facilitating environment, and what Winnicott called "transitional phenomena." As we saw in Chapter Two, online spaces can offer a particular kind of interactive environment that makes space for children to play with their identities as they develop through a variety of developmental stages (Clarke, 2009). While the following chapter will examine how processes of identity play and development are activated across SNSs, the *space* in which identity and other psychodynamics are processed and expressed will be investigated here.

The SNS offers a particular kind of space for children, young people, and adults to explore both their identities and the nature of their intersubjective spaces in much the same way that Winnicott (1971) describes how infant's play is a symbolic *and* practical exploration of their limits under the guidance of their care-takers in the context of their holding within the facilitating environment. This play enables the infant to feel through the important transitional state between her sense of omnipotence and her relationship to the real world, which is limited. These limits operate on a variety of different levels from the fundamental limits of the physical body, to those of the physical environment and the emotional and psychological limits of themselves and their care-takers. Relationally speaking, they are to do with the extensions of the self and the extensions of others in intersubjective space. While the activity in this space is often referred to as "play", there is a great deal of important working through occurring here in relation to the developing sense of self (real and false) and the development of object relations: the incorporation or introjection of the mother or primary care-taker into the psyche of the infant herself.

Because the play that occurs in the facilitating environment between the infant and mother is composed of transitional phenomena that comprise elements that are both "me" and "not me", Winnicott (1971) uses the word "magical" to describe this playing in potential space:

> The thing about playing is always the precariousness of the interplay of personal psychic reality and the experience of control of actual objects. This is the precariousness of magic itself, magic that arises in intimacy, in a relationship that is being found to be reliable. (p. 47)

Through good-enough mothering, the infant is able to reach out into the world and begin to encounter its reality—a reality that necessitates an undermining of his omnipotence. Through this play, the mother allows the child, for a period at least, to maintain an illusion that he is omnipotent and that his mother's breast is under his own magical control, almost as if it were a part of himself. The developmental task at this stage is twofold, including both separation from the quasi-symbiosis with his mother and recognition of his mother's subjectivity as separate from himself. Both of these tasks necessitate an encounter between his omnipotent sense of self and the reality of the other, ideally concluding in the loss of omnipotence and the gaining of a self among others. In later life, omnipotence (which is related to narcissism) is an axis upon which we all operate, sometimes allowing ourselves to be affected by others, and other times resistant to that impact by unconsciously trying to impose our own will on others: for example, by not allowing their influence to seem important to us. The need for, and expression of, omnipotence never completely cease and its activation usually provokes both frustration and anxiety. Online interaction, which is engaged through the filter of false self and persona (because of the SNS's "outward-facing" function) enables some degree of omnipotence because it allows the user to control what happens in their interface and achieve psychological distance if necessary. At the same time, this interface works the other way around, making users present online and open to impact from others and, thereby, challenging their sense of omnipotence through their vulnerability to virtual impingement. This particular zone of private and public, this transitional space offered to us by the virtual environment, is deftly described by Turkle (2011):

at a screen, you feel protected and less burdened by expectations. And, although you are alone, the potential for almost instantaneous contact gives an encouraging feeling of already being together. In this curious relational space, even sophisticated users who know that electronic communications can be saved, shared, and show up in court, succumb to its illusion of privacy. Alone with your thoughts, yet in contact with an almost tangible fantasy of the other, you feel free to play. At the screen, you have a chance to write yourself into the person you want to be and to imagine others as you wish them to be, constructing them for your purposes. It is a seductive but dangerous habit of mind. (p. 187)

In this sense, it becomes clear how this space offers a different context to most others; it offers at the same time a sense of remove and a sense of closeness; a sense of privacy and a sense of public exposure; a sense of proximity and a sense of distance.

The paradoxical nature of this space is resonant with the original sense of holding in the facilitating environment that encourages the developmental trajectory towards a self–other relation in which the infant moves from perceiving the other subjectively (that is, as an extension of himself), to the more highly developed position where the other is, as Winnicott (1986) puts it, "objectively perceived"[26] (p. 256). No doubt there is no way that one can really and truly objectively perceive another—it is important to distinguish the developmental shift in self-perception with its movement from seeing the other as an aspect of the self ("he or she is the same as me") to their being seen as a subject in their own right ("he or she is different from me"). The way in which another is subjectively perceived is akin to narcissism and omnipotence, while the way in which one is objectively perceived is akin to mutual recognition. In another paper, Winnicott (1969) puts it this way, which unfortunately also invites some terminological confusion: that is, the distinction between object relating (akin to the object subjectively perceived) and object use (akin to the object objectively perceived). In Winnicott's words, "the *relating* can be described in terms of the individual subject, and that *usage* cannot be described except in terms of acceptance of the object's independent existence" (p. 712). Recognising that Winnicott's language is rather confusingly worded, particularly because the word "usage" has pejorative resonances, Benjamin (1988) paraphrases beautifully and simply:

At first, Winnicott says, an object is 'related' to, it is part of the subject's mind and not necessarily experienced as real, external, or independent. But there comes a point in the subject's development where this kind of relatedness must give way to an appreciation of the object as an outside entity, not merely something in one's mind. This ability to enter into exchange with the outside object is what Winnicott calls 'using' the object. (p. 37)

The trajectory that both Winnicott and Benjamin are describing here is a movement into intersubjective space, the bursting of the illusion of omnipotence with limits of the world, and the difference of others. In the object-relating condition, the infant sees the other as an object subjectively perceived. When he moves to object usage, he is able to see the other as a full subject "objectively perceived", that is, not a part of himself, but another person in his or her own right. This process is not an immediate one, and neither is it one that ever happens completely. In moving from point A to point B, the infant experiences an "intermediate area of experience" as Winnicott (1986) describes:

> *The intermediate area to which I am referring is the area that is allowed to the infant between primarily creativity and objective perception based on reality testing.* The transitional phenomena represent the early stages of the use of illusion, without which there is no meaning for the human being in the idea of a relationship with an object that is perceived by another as external to that being. (p. 266, original italics)

The use of the words "magic" earlier and "illusion" here are important, as we try to conceptualise the idea that online social networks have the capacity to occupy a similar transitional space for us in these same magical and illusionary ways, activating our omnipotent fantasies and the working-through of how we see others (and ourselves) on a spectrum of objectivity and subjectivity (in Winnicott's sense): as objects and as subjects. Although Winnicott is describing early infant experience, the *dynamics* involved in the dialectical relationship between internal reality and external reality continue throughout life as we carry on working through transitional space in all of our relationships with others.

Consider these elements of transitional phenomena in the context of interaction over an online social network. One is alone, but virtually one is with others. One maintains a certain degree of omnipotence that does not exist in the hard reality of everyday life. For example, if another person on an SNS is bothersome, we can prevent them from appearing in our newsfeed. At will, one can engage at a very deep level, for example through synchronous communication over Facebook chat, or operate on the shallowest level by way of clicking the "like" button on someone's profile. One can allow oneself to be affected profoundly by the communication of another, for example, by a contrary opinion expressed under one's status that may be experienced as an attack, or one can divert one's attention from potential virtual impingement simply by clicking another hyperlink. Unconsciously, however, the impingement remains, as does the original cause of it in cyberspace. In this fashion, cyberspace itself works like the unconscious, remembering every-thing, while consciousness retains only what is currently on the screen. The SNS offers us a transitional space where the alone-but-not-alone works through or gets stuck in the dynamics of omnipotence or mutual recognition. The possibilities along this spectrum are wide, and perhaps this is part of what compels so many to engage with SNSs. The positively regressive nature of the omnipotence is richly enjoyed, though it is highly defensive. However, one also retains the ability to regulate interaction, to move into object relating or object use, to allow oneself to subjectively perceive the object or to objec-tively perceive the subject, to discover the other and to be discovered. In relation to online relating, these dynamics are fully operational at all sorts of levels; Lingiardi (2011) puts it thus:

> computer-mediated communication allows the user to play with real-ities and identities. It can thus contain transitional elements as defined by Winnicott; the transitional object, in fact, lies halfway between Me and not-Me, between reality and fantasy, between near and far, between what we create and what we discover. Serving as a potential space between subject and environment (a space for experimenting with the Self between me and myself, and between me and the other), the online experience—which in many cases facilitates and feeds dissociation—can also help us illuminate the difficult path between separation anxiety and being engulfed by the object. (p. 487)

The dialectic between the internal and external world persists from the infant's earliest days, in which she is completely dependent on her primary care-takers, to that phase where separation and individuation becomes the central task. Lingiardi, above, relates these experiences to transitional elements, notably the transitional object. For Winnicott, the transitional object is the magical object *par excellence* because it occupies an "intermediate area between the subjective and that which is objectively perceived" (1986, p. 256). This transitional object accomplishes a great deal of work in shepherding the developing infant's mind from an internal world to a full participant in the external world; it is crucial in the development of symbolism and symbolic thinking:

> When symbolism is employed the infant is already clearly distinguishing between fantasy and fact, between inner object and external objects, between primary creativity and perception . . . the term transitional object . . . gives room for the process of becoming able to accept difference and similarity . . . a term that describes the infant's journey from the purely subjective to objectivity . . . the transitional object . . . is what we see of this journey of progress towards experiencing. (Winnicott, 1985, p. 259)

I posit that the presentation of the *self* online operates like a transitional object in the transitional space that is the online social network. The self is opened up as an object under the gaze of others— it is "me" (or at least a representation of me) and it is at the same time "not me" because it is out there in transitional space. Once it is outside the psyche and online, it falls outside one's control, no matter how much care went into that original presentation. It becomes "like me" but "not me". With regard to SNSs, the virtual transitional object of the self is an entity created by the self (with the particular activation of the false self, or persona) and launched into virtual space; this is an active extension of self despite the lack of control that commences after the object is thrust into virtual space. Contrarily, the cobbled-together identity that appears online by way of a Google search is a passive object representation of the self in the virtual world. This passive accumulation of "self parts" occupies the transitional space of the Internet in a different way, as it is not composed by way of a purposeful representation of the self; it does, however, still represent a reflection of that self (to the subject and to others) that is likely to remain online within one's permanent data trail. While the consequences for identity will be discussed in the following chapter, the presence of an image of self online continues to operate on a number

of different psychodynamic levels, obviously inclusive of the objectification of the subject, the nature of recognition, and how one remains
as an image in the mind of the other, virtually, however accurate
(objectively perceived) that image may be.

All of these elements combine to create a tension of the self as it
appears online. There is always a dialectic of subject and object,
omnipotence and limit. These are reflective of the self-same developmental tensions in the original transitional space created by a facilitating environment that may or may not be "good enough." A good
enough environment enables a positive recognition of self by the
other, and vice versa, allowing for the subject to be both in intersubjective space with others, and to be alone without being lonely. As we
have seen in Chapter Three, this is what Winnicott (1982c) refers to as
"The capacity to be alone". By developing a capacity to be alone, the
child develops a sense of trust that things are all right when he is
alone because he has internalised the supportive love of his primary
care-taker in a way that is sustaining even when that care-taker is no
longer there. This is a Winicottian development of Klein's (1946)
thinking on the developmental achievement of the depressive position, where the infant learns to relate to whole objects in a non-
schizoid or persecutory way. Benjamin (1988) develops Winnnicott's
idea further, noting that in the intersubjective paradigm, "the relationship between self and other, with its tension between sameness
and difference . . . [is] a continual exchange of influence. It focuses, not
on a linear movement from oneness to separateness, but on the paradoxical balance between them" (p. 49). SNSs embody this paradox
and the way in which an individual engages with them will be dependent upon their internal object relations and their interpersonal relational structures and needs. Importantly, the templates for these are
laid down long before an individual first encounters an online social
network. The popular notion that SNSs *cause* a trait like narcissism, for
example, makes little sense from a developmental perspective.

In order to be an active subject in the social world, one has to
manage not only the capacity to be alone, but also the capacity to be
with others; the SNS can be utilised either way. Both Benjamin and
Winnicott understand these dialectics between self and other, omnipotence and limit testing, sameness and difference, as relational challenges that continue throughout the life cycle; the way in which we
are likely to manage these dialectics is predicated by early experience.

While it is clear that the way in which an older child or adolescent plays with identity across an SNS and the way an infant navigates potential space in early play with the mother are quite different, the dynamics of the earlier infantile play underlie similar activities in later life. The way in which we navigate both aloneness and togetherness is very much modelled on our internal object relations, which is profoundly connected to how we manage loss.

Defending against loss

One of the paradoxes of online social networking is the fact that the extensions of ourselves, as mediated through it, can be actively present and absent at the same time, for even when we are not online our profiles remain present to others despite our absence from a computer terminal or a smartphone. The same is true for those others who remain present to us by way of *their* online profiles no matter where they are, whether or not they are online, whether they are alive or dead. A prime case of this was exemplified through my own clinical experience with Thomas, as I described in Chapter Two. Thomas was looking for a representation of me during a time when I was absent from him in real life. In his object relational desire to pull up an image of me in his mind, he chose to do so online. In this case, Thomas was responding to the feelings of absence or loss he was having in relation to his anxious emotional state; he was looking for a good object. The nature of loss is absolutely central to how we conceive of how one remains in the mind of the other. While a big loss such as the ending of an intimate relationship or the death of a loved one provides particular challenges for an individual, loss is a process in which we engage every day, whether it is the loss of our omnipotence, as described above, or the absence of an important other. Freud's work on loss can be seen retrospectively as one of the paradigmatic shifts in original psychoanalytic theory that would eventually lead to the theoretical development of object relations and later relational theory, as was described in Chapter One. It was the development of the idea of "the object" as it appears in Freud's essay "Mourning and melancholia" (1917e) that shifted thinking from a purely drive-based psychoanalytic model of the psyche (libido theory) towards an object relational one. It will be necessary to digress here for a moment into

Freud's theory of mourning and melancholia, before applying it to the material at hand.

In this essay, Freud draws out the distinction between the related processes of mourning and melancholia (grief and depression) in relation to something (usually a person) that has been lost. In his theorising, however, he also shifts psychoanalytic theory towards recognising how others in our lives, through the process of identification, become part of our own psyches, a process that has become crucial to our understanding of both identity development and how object relations and intersubjectivity develop across the lifespan. Implicit in his theory lies the notion that we are not individuals with "one psychology" (Aron, 1996), living among others, but unreservedly and intimately connected to those others in the very development of our subjectivities. Both mourning and melancholia are responses to a lost or absent person—what is referred to in the jargon as the "lost object".

In mourning, we are required to withdraw our psychic energy (libido) from the object, the psychic energy that we have invested in the other with such care. This is the painful process of loss, and through it we come to recover from the pain of it and are able to love again; a new object can come along and we have freed some fresh libido to invest in that. Contrastingly, in melancholia, we find that we are unable to let go of that object that has, in reality, gone. Unconsciously, we bring that object inside of ourselves and hold on to it, refusing to let it go; our ambivalent relationship to the external object continues unabated within ourselves, a process of loving and hating the object that ultimately causes the depression. Whereas in mourning the libido is released from the lost object, thereby making room for the new one, in melancholia, libido sticks to the old object as it remains represented inside our own psyche. In some of Freud's most famous words, he describes how, in response to the loss of the other, "the shadow of the object fell upon the ego, and the latter could henceforth be judged by a special agency, as though it were an object, the forsaken object" (Freud, 1917e, p. 249). This shadow is the internalised representation of the external object that has now been introjected; the object is retained within the ego itself. The ego now contains both the forsaken object, and that other part of the ego he refers to as the "special agency" (he later develops this concept into the superego) that observes and judges this new object within the ego. It is the nature of the harsh judgement of the superego that causes the depression as the ambivalence and judgement previously targeted at the external object are now targeted at the self. The ego is now multiple, containing its original architecture and the new part, the shadow of the lost object, which becomes a part of it. In this Freud is describing the nature of identification in which the ego itself is altered by its identification with the lost object.

When we trace the notion of identification further, we find that in Freud's later writings, such as *The Ego and the Id* (1923b), and in particular in post-Freudian theorists such as Klein, Fairbairn, Winnicott, and others, identification occurs as a matter of course in the *normal development of the psyche*, not just as response to loss. As we saw in Chapter One, all of these theorists took an active part in shifting psychoanalysis from a libidinal drive theory towards a focus on the motivation to relate (Greenberg & Mitchell, 1983). Fairbairn (1944), for example, described human subjectivity as fundamentally object-seeking, while later theorists such as Bowlby (Holmes, 1993) and Winnicott, in their own unique ways, would further develop the theory of the object in relation to attachment and the infant–mother relationship. As we shall see, these object relational dynamics are always at play in an individual's use of the online social network.

The salient feature of all these divergent theories is that the object (the mental representation of the other) is brought inside the psyche and *alters the ego itself* by its presence. When Freud describes the mourning process, he explains that as the attachment to the object is abandoned (psychically), "every single one of the memories and expectations in which the libido is bound to the object is brought up and hyper-cathected"[27] (1917e, p. 245). Here, Freud is describing the highly emotional feelings we experience in grieving when we remember events we shared with our lost loved one, or experience new events in which we think of them. In a sense, Freud is saying that these memories and expectations act like internal objects in which we invest emotional energy. From this perspective, we may approach "objects" as represented across online social networks as also being capable of all the actions and dynamics described within the processes of mourning and melancholia. The question that arises in this perspective, then, is whether or not the online social networking world is melancholic in nature because there never really is a loss: the *other* is always findable online. Another question arises with regard to the nature of the outsourcing quality of relationships as they occur online.

If the object remains "out there", what are the psychological conse-quences "in here", within the psyche? There are a variety of ways in which we can look at the functionality of SNSs in regard to these ques-tions. While relationship break-ups will be utilised here to apply the theory of mourning and loss to online functioning, these dynamics are at play on a number of different levels.[28] Marshall's (2012) research on the nature of relationships that break up across Facebook sheds some light on these questions. In her review of previous research on the effects of SNSs on romantic relationships, Marshall notes that

> frequent monitoring of an ex-partner's Facebook page and list of friends, even when one was not a Facebook friend of the ex-partner, was associated with greater current distress over the breakup, nega-tive feelings, sexual desire, longing for the ex-partner and lower personal growth. (p. 5)

The online environment offers different challenges to the psyche with regard to loss, in that interaction can occur passively by way of acci-dentally witnessing what an ex might be getting up to through a news feed, or actively by engaging in what is often called "Facebook stalk-ing". Online psychological experiences with regard to loss (or the inability to accept loss) has offline repercussions as well, as Lyndon, Bonds-Raake, and Cratty (2011) found:

> Monitoring an ex-partner's Facebook photos and other forms of covert provocation (such as writing a status update to make an ex-partner jealous) is associated with an increased likelihood of engaging in offline obsessive relational intrusion (e.g., showing up at the ex-part-ner's classroom or workplace). (cited in Marshall, 2012, p. 2)

These sorts of experiences fall straight into Freud's model of hyper-cathecting each of the "memories and expectations" associated with the lost object. In this case, the accumulation of energy and the obsessive revisiting of the object as it remains online in cyberspace exacerbates the energetic system, causing acting out online. However, Marshall's findings also brought up some contradictory information. As we have seen from other research, quantitative statistical methods based on survey responses often throw up anomalies because they do not ask users questions about their experiences as a more phenome-nological approach might. In this case, the survey responses indicated that

... people who remained Facebook friends with an ex-partner were lower in negative feelings, sexual desire and longing for the former partner than people who were not Facebook friends ... [there is the possibility that] unbidden exposure to the potentially banal status updates, comments, and photos of an ex-partner through remaining Facebook friends may have decreased any residual attraction to the ex-partner. (p. 5)

In this alternative case, remaining "friends" with a partner actually aided the Facebook user to feel less romantically inclined towards them. Marshall offers this explanation:

Former partners with whom we are no longer in contact ... may remain shrouded in an alluring mystique, suggesting that remaining Facebook friends with an ex-partner may actually help rather than harm one's breakup recovery. (Marshall, 2012, p. 5)

As other personality-based research has found, people are likely to engage across the online network in the style of their personalities (as we saw in the previous chapter). With regard to the model proposed in this text, individuals will engage in their online relationships in ways that their relational style dictates in synergy with what the online social network allows. In this case, a person whose relational style leans towards a more melancholic model (that is, the lack of an ability to let the object go) will be more likely to engage in Facebook stalking in an effort to retain the lost object in consciousness by way of online tracking. On the other side of the equation, we can surmise that there might be some purpose to the way in which an ex-partner may present their life online with the very purpose of remaining in the mind of the other (the partner who was left), thereby retaining some sort of virtual intersubjective connection: another example of a melancholic holding on to the lost object rather than letting it go from the other person's point of view. It is important to keep in mind that the ease of online tracking invites anyone on the SNS to engage in behaviours that they may have, in other circumstances, avoided. The ease and convenience of tracking an ex enables this behaviour even in individuals whose relational styles may not ordinarily seek such a relationship to the lost object. Marshall (2012) saw fit to conclude her research with some frank advice,

> keeping tabs on an ex-partner through Facebook is associated with poorer emotional recovery and personal growth following a breakup. Therefore, avoiding exposure to an ex-partner, both offline and online, may be the best remedy for healing a broken heart. (p. 6)

This conclusion is applicable far beyond the nature of online break-ups and functions centrally in the way that relationships are negotiated in an online environment. Furthermore, the conclusion clearly resonates with Freud's model of mourning, suggesting that the mourning process is better worked through when one does not maintain an online object relationship with the former lover. Here, we have a further extension of the unconscious relational structure online, in which a variety of different relationships operate in that transitional space between the object being "out there" and "in here", consistently working through our internal object relational selves within real and virtual intersubjective spaces. In fact, the distinction between *real* and *virtual* spaces becomes blurred in the context of *intersubjective space*, because intersubjective space happens *between* two minds in any case, a meeting in *psychological space* that occurs neither in the arena of the virtual or the real world: it is an intra and interpsychic phenomenon. While the architecture of an SNS such as Facebook enables the *being in the mind of the other* in more accessible ways at all hours of the day, it also offers a rather melancholic relationship to others, ultimately affecting *letting go* and freely enabling an ongoing defence against loss. The availability, ease, and convenience of this extension of ourselves into online virtual transitional space has become the very nature of our contemporary relational lives and activities online.

Facebook relationships are an extension of real relationships

Of all SNSs, Facebook presents itself as an important exemplar of an SNS operating in transitional space, not only because it is the most popular SNS in the world, indicating that it is wildly attractive to people across the globe, but also because Facebook relationships, for the most part, are extensions of real relationships that exist offline. An abundance of research indicates that most Facebook relationships originated in real offline social networks. For example, Lampe, Ellison, and Steinfield's (2006) study of first year University students in the USA concludes that their subjects primarily use Facebook for maintaining previous relationships or looking into individuals that they meet offline: as a rule they do not tend to use Facebook to meet new people. This finding was confirmed by Hampton, Goulet, Rainie, and Purcell's (2011) large-scale study for the *Pew Internet and American Life Project*, which concluded that not only did Facebook allow users to keep in better touch with close ties, but also enabled them to revive dormant relationships. Greene (2012) sums up some of the Pew research nicely:

> Far from confirming that Facebook atomised and isolated its users . . . [the research] found that they had about 9% more strong offline social ties than non-users [an effect not isolated to Facebook, but other online social networks too]. Facebook users were more likely to agree that 'most people can be trusted'. And they have more diverse social networks—counter to the claim that social networking facilitates social bubbles. (p. 76)

The feeling that "most people can be trusted" (Hampton, Goulet, Rainie, & Purcell, 2011, p. 4) is a particularly interesting finding because it relates precisely to the dynamics discussed above with regard to early experience and the good enough facilitating environment which enables trust in the external world. The failure of this environment results in a leaning towards what Klein (1935) called the paranoid–schizoid position, in which the external world remains hostile and persecutory. This psychological position is a fundamental component of adult mistrust of others and the external world, as it is a reflection of an original and profound mistrust of the immediate facilitating environment instigated by the not-good-enough primary care-taker.[29] The prevalence of those who trust others on Facebook is curious and provokes the question of whether Facebook is attracting those who already retain a trust in others and the world, or whether the transitional space that Facebook offers can actually engender warmer object relations to others in the external world.

Because Facebook extends our already existing offline networks and relocates them online, it offers a virtual transitional space that facilitates the ease and frequency of engagement with multiple people at one time; an activity that engages intersubjective activity with a variety of weak and strong ties. The average number of Facebook friends tends to vary according to studies. Pew's research (Hampton, Goulet, Rainie, & Purcell, 2011), for example, came out with the number of average friends at 229 (p. 5) while Ugander, Karrer, Backstrom, and Marlow (2011) found a statistical average of around 190. The study by Ugander et al. is likely to be more accurate, as it was a massive quantitative analysis carried out on Facebook itself, while the Pew research consists of a sample of under a thousand individuals. As a small number of individuals will have a disproportionate number of friends in the region of the 5000 maximum, averages may not be representative of the "average user". The problem with the large-scale studies, as previously discussed, is that they give little, if any, information about how users manage and perceive their "friends" across the network; something that is a complex and thoughtful operation carried out by users, as Marlow (2009) suggests. None the less, it is interesting to find that the averages lie just above the range of the number Dunbar offers as the limit of social relationships that can be maintained in an individual's mind at any one time, generally conceived to be around 150, give or take (Dunbar, 1998). While, of course, many individuals have more friends than this, Marlow (2009) has shown that not all Facebook friends are equal; an individual tends to stay in regular contact with a small grouping of "maintained friends" despite a much larger cohort of friends present on their profile. In this light, we can see how Facebook operates as a sort of contact management tool, rather than as a whole "new" way of online social relating.

The study carried out by Hampton, Goulet, Rainie, and Purcell (2011) provides an exhaustive amount of information about social networking use, with particular attention to Facebook (the social network upon which 92% of social network users in the survey used). The researchers surveyed 2,255 Americans, most of whom were Internet users (n=1787) and less than half were SNS users (n=975). The authors acknowledge from the start that people use online social networks for a variety of reasons, which, of course, cannot all be accounted for in their research. However, using their survey data in relation to their earlier report on social isolation (Hampton, Sessions, Her, & Rainie, 2009) offers us a good deal of insight, particularly their finding that "Facebook use seems to support intimacy, rather than undermine it" (p. 25). Let us examine some of the details of this report in reference to other similar research.

First of all, who are Facebook friends? The Pew research found categories of friends break down into the following, in order of most to least: friends from high school; extended family; co-workers; college friends; immediate family; voluntary groups and neighbours. A full 31%, however, defy classification, and of those that defy classification, a mere 7% are those the user has never met in person and 3% those whom they have met only once. The rest are friends of friends (p. 5). These numbers show us that Facebook is primarily used as a utility to maintain relationships that are already existent, and we can extrapolate that the number of maintained relationships, rather than the number of friends as a whole, is likely to fall within Dunbar's number of around 150. Even new relationships are generally founded upon friends of friends, hence Facebook networks are nearly fully connected, as also demonstrated by Ugander, Karrer, Backstrom, and Marlow (2011). Interestingly, users engage with Facebook in more subtle and complex ways then they are often given credit for. For example, both weak and strong ties are attended to differently across the network (Backstrom, Bakshy, Kleinberg, Lento, & Rosenn, 2011). Bakshy (2012), one of the researchers on the previously mentioned study, notes that while people are most likely to share information across their strongest ties on Facebook, the fear that "social networks are echo chambers" is disproven by the research: in fact,

> the vast majority of information comes from contacts that they interact with infrequently. These distant contacts are also more likely to share novel information, demonstrating that social networks can act as a powerful medium for sharing new ideas . . . [and] may actually increase the spread of novel information and diverse viewpoints.

By unpacking this, we learn that although close ties are more highly maintained and interacted with online, ties that are further afield (friends of friends, for example) are able to affect the nature of social bubbles with novel thoughts and ideas. This finding is further evidence of the capacity of Facebook to engender the *being in the mind of the other* from further afield and by way of feelings and ideas rather than just personal relationships. Hampton, Goulet, Rainie, and Purcell (2011) report that 40% of SNS users (mostly on Facebook) have friended all of their closest confidants, noting that individuals use SNSs "increasingly . . . to keep up with close social ties" (p. 5); in other words, to keep others in mind, and to passively or actively remain in the minds of others. The facility and ease of Facebook use and its reliance on previously created offline relationships has a series of consequences that the Pew study concludes are all rather positive, including the point made above that Facebook users are more trusting than others (a full 43% more likely to agree "that most people can be trusted" than those who use the Internet but are not on Facebook[30]) and that they get more social support than others (p. 4). With regard to trust, Valenzuela, Park, and Kee (2009) note that it is unlikely that Facebook users would keep others on their lists whom they would not trust, in which case

> Facebook usage could be positively correlated to having online networks of likeable and trusting members. Likewise, believing that others will not knowingly harm us may facilitate usage of online network services. In other words, social trust and Facebook use may have a reciprocal relationship. (p. 878)

These findings seem to support not only my argument that the online social network is like a facilitating environment, but also that individual online social networks are unconsciously organised to be "good enough" and supportive of positive relational interdependence. There is even a fair chance that the online social network, in supporting the "being in the mind of the other" in transitional space, can offer a reparative experience (as long-term psychotherapy does) to remediate earlier relational environments that were not "good enough". In reference to research carried out in 2008 on social isolation (Hampton, Sessions, Her, & Rainie, 2009), the 2011 Pew report found that Americans reported having more close friends than in the earlier research, as well as finding a significant decrease (from 12% to 9%) in those that reported that "they had no one with whom they could discuss important matters" (Hampton, Goulet, Rainie, & Purcell, 2011, p. 24). While this cannot be directly related to the concurrent rise in the number of people using Facebook, we can, none the less, extrapolate that its ease of use, alongside its proven ability to support intimacy, may have had something to do with this significant decrease in such a short period of time. In summarising their findings, Hampton, Goulet, Rainie, and Purcell (2011) note that after we control for demographic characteristics, we do not find that use of any SNS platform is associated with having a larger or smaller general overall social network. However, we do find that Facebook users are more likely to have a larger number of close social ties. (p. 25)

As we have seen in this section, the way in which Facebook friends are managed is complex, varied, and thoughtful. Echoing Burkeman's (2012) concerns about friends being seen as clutter, discussed in the previous chapter, the blogger, Chris Baraniuk (2011) notes the cultural discomfort with the loss of the meaning of the word "friend":

> One of the most frequent complaints people make about Facebook and other social networking services is they feel that it detracts from or displaces more traditional and more meaningful engagement with their friends in face-to-face scenarios . . . the meaning of the word 'friend' has been fundamentally *blurred* by Facebook's architecture. People, no wonder, are left confused. (Baraniuk, 2011)

While this concern is frequently the subject of popular discussion, it seems less of an issue for those who actually engage with their friends across social networks. This is clear from the work done by Bryant and Marmo (2012), which suggests that Facebook users do not find their friends in a muddle (or in a way that is "blurred" by the architecture of Facebook, to draw on Baraniuk's view). Instead, they make conscious distinctions between their Facebook friends by placing them into broad categories such as "close friends, casual friends, and acquaintances" (p. 6). By way of a two-pronged qualitative research project, Bryant and Marmo (2012) sought to find what implicit rules might be directing these relationships. The first phase of their research arrived at thirty-six rules, which were then reduced by way of focus group endorsements of the most salient ones, ultimately resulting in the five most important rules:

> I should expect a response from this person if I post on his/her profile.
>
> I should not say anything disrespectful about this person.
>
> I should consider how a post might negatively impact this person's relationships.
>
> If I post something this person deletes, I should not repost it.
>
> I should communicate with this person outside of Facebook (Bryant & Marmo, 2012, p. 12)

A thematic reading of these five rules indicate a strong leaning towards respect of the other's subjectivity, sensitivity, and care towards another's needs, and a necessary capacity for empathy and the ability to keep the mind and sensibility of other users in mind. These findings go further to support the enhanced trust that was found in Hampton, Goulet, Rainie, and Purcell's (2011) research, and further supports the idea that Facebook can, and often does, offer a "good enough" facilitating environment that may enhance trust. Interestingly, Bryant and Marmo (2012) also found that

> Concerning the endorsement of relational maintenance rules, acquaintances and casual friends did not significantly differ from each other, yet both reported significantly greater endorsement of relational maintenance rules than did close friends. (p. 18)

While this finding seemed to contradict earlier research that had indicated that close friends seemed to utilise more maintenance rules than casual relationships, from the psychodynamic perspective this makes sense. Because the relational structures operating between close friends who meet offline will be stronger, it would make sense that the *implicit* rules between strong ties will indeed be stronger, operating more unconsciously and outside immediate conscious thought. Because there is less of a historic offline intersubjective tie between casual friends and acquaintances, there will be more concern about how these less trusted relationships should be handled, so, indeed, they are handled with more care and *conscious* or *explicit* rule-following. In fact, although Bryant and Marmo argue that this contradictory finding needs more research, their own study seems to support why casual friends and acquaintances require more conscious maintenance rules, "the present study suggests that Facebook friends are highly concerned about the appropriateness of various communication channels as well as the importance of facework and impression management" (2012, p. 17). Facework, in many ways, is the sociological correlate to persona,

> Face is an image of self delineated in terms of approved social attribute—albeit an image that others may share, as when a person makes a good showing for his profession or religion by making a good showing of himself. (Goffman, 1955, p. 451)

In this sense, facework, or persona, is more important in retaining connections to weak ties (remaining in the mind of the other *in a particular way*) than it is with regard to stronger ties with whom the user does not have to work so hard because they are more secure, so that they remain safely in the mind of the other. This is reminiscent of the aphorism, "Friends: people who know you well, but like you anyway". The friends, in this aphorism, are obviously the close tie, close friend variety. It seems as if, whatever nature a friendship retains, Facebook users are making these distinctions and acting accordingly. Facebook operates like an online extension of real offline relationships, an outsourced data-pool that keeps others in mind while keeping the user in the minds of others. In this way, though intersubjective, it is also rather melancholic (in the Freudian sense) and may disrupt the capacity to be alone.

Little reminders that I am here, like stones thrown at a window

Throughout this text, I have been drawing on psychoanalytic know-ledge originally derived from the clinic in an effort to tease out the related psychodynamics that I believe are fundamentally activated by the online social networking environment. In Chapter Two, I drew upon my own clinical experience to extrapolate similar dynamics occurring outside the clinic. Lingiardi (2008), in a similar fashion, reflects on how his patient, "Melania", sent him an email in order to remain in his mind during the summer holiday break from her psychoanalysis. By sending this email, she

> walked out of the door of my office but then she figured out how to come in through the 'window' of my computer! . . . By sending an email message, the patient can act on the desire to drag the analyst away from the rules of the setting, which she/he experiences, uncon-sciously or not, as a restriction on unconditional love and availability. (pp. 112–113)

Lingiardi goes on to describe the continued used of emails in the ther-apy in suggesting, by way of a rather beautiful metaphor, that his patient's emails, in this sense, were like "Pebbles marking the path between one session and the next, marking the way home like the kid in the fairy-tale did. Pebbles to fill a void and lay out a path" (p. 113). And these pebbles were found to be more than that,

> her emails weren't just pebbles tossed on the ground to help find her path in analysis; they were also 'pebbles thrown *against* the window of the analysis room', in order to keep me alive and awake . . . They were pebbles meant to ensure that I, too, didn't lose sight of the path of the analysis and of herself. (Lingiardi, 2008, p. 113)

Throughout this experience, Lingiardi learned how technology is used in relation to the clinical encounter to remain in the mind of the other.

Psychoanalyst Evan Malater (2007b) uses rich Lacanian language to work through how the boundary-challenging nature of technology raps at the door of therapeutic boundaries. He notes how it is the therapist's rather difficult job to work out his or her role in relation to electronic communication such as an email:

> The act of reading an e-mail puts a therapist in front of a conversation that both did and did not happen with others who are both there and not there in a space that is both there and not there. Feeling a peculiar blurring of boundaries and the queasy sense of the uncanny, the therapists struggles to regain solid footing on the ground of the Symbolic to the pull of the Real. For a moment, the therapist is transported in to the archives of the patient's life, granted the power to examine the objective past, and called upon to make judgements. (p 166)

As described in Chapter Three, the therapeutic relationship and the presence of "the third" allows the therapist (with whatever difficulty) to navigate this uncanny experience between boundaries with their patients. Even in this particular therapeutic space, this is not easy. Within these clinical situations, we again find ourselves with a parallel that we can apply to intersubjectivity between individuals across the online social network. The way in which Lingiardi's patient wished to remain in his mind via her emails, the way Malater describes the effect of the "peculiar blurring of boundaries", or the way in which Thomas (from Chapter Two) sought, in his way, to grasp on to an image of me by way of a Google search, are clinical representations of what I hypothesise is going on all the time on social networks. Across the online social network, we are both objectified and subjectified; we seek recognition for our true selves while being compelled to present our false selves; we struggle with intrapsychic object relations while seeking the satisfaction of intersubjective interaction. The online social networking environment, alongside other operations of the Internet in general, provides a transitional space in which this work occurs. This work is occurring down to the very level of our identities, which are more and more becoming expressed both on and offline.

CHAPTER SIX

Identities are not virtual

"I thereby concluded that I was a substance, of which the whole essence or nature consists in thinking, and which, in order to exist, needs no place and depends on no material thing; so that this 'I', that is to say, the mind, by which I am what I am, is entirely distinct from the body, and even that it is easier to know than the body . . ."

(Descartes, 1637)

In the introduction to this text, I posed the question: "Is the development of what has come to be called 'Web 2.0' changing us in some fundamental way, or is it simply a novel technological platform through which the same old psychological traits express themselves through a different medium?" It is my hope that the previous chapters have gone some way in enabling us to come closer to an answer to this question. So far, we have seen how the same relational psychodynamics that underlie offline relationships are at play across online social networks; these online social networks and accompanying technologies (smartphones, tablets, and the ubiquity of 3G and now 4G networks) that saturate our daily lives are posing additional opportunities and challenges to the way in which these psychodynamics are at play. The convenience of access to others in conjunction with the architecture of SNSs has a series of consequences with regard to the nature of our intimate and not-so-intimate relating. More and more, our internal and external worlds are merged as aspects of ourselves are present online twenty-four hours a day. As a result, we are, at the same time, made more accessible than ever before, but also more relationally distracted because we all share in this accessibility. The way in which individuals choose to relate to each other over SNSs is as diverse as the architecture of their platforms allows. Across SNSs, we can engage as extraverts or introverts, as voyeurs or as exhibitionists, as honest expressions of our selves (as we understand that to be), or as a well-honed persona. These choices are dependent, of course, on proclivities, psychodynamics, and personality styles; although SNSs may encourage certain kinds of relating, the *nature* of the identities of those who are relating across them is not "virtual"; it is a real identity expressed over a digital medium.

The representations of ourselves that we choose to put online comprise different aspects of our multiple psyches in relation to the imagined and real audiences that we encounter through SNSs. Those multiply constructed, cobbled-together identities are not isolated chimeras operating in a virtual fantasy world; rather, they are fundamentally informed by our subjectivities performing important psychodynamic functions within the intersubjective matrix, involving the way in which we see ourselves, the way in which we wish to see ourselves (our ego ideals), the way we wish others to see us, as well as those parts of ourselves that we may wish to remain out of sight all together. The same holds true for those that we seek online; they themselves are virtually composed of the same materials, from the accretions of information collected by Google in the passive fashion as described in Chapter Two to the more purposeful active presentation of self deployed across SNSs. From these online identities, we get some information, but there is more room for projection and transference than there is in real life because the online presence exists outside of full intersubjective containment and outside the psychoanalytic third. What results is an interpersonal space that is available as an online representation of a self that is instantaneous yet multiple, sometimes lacking in depth, and presented to us in many pieces.

Developmentally digital: Native and Immigrant

The way in which we are all, to various degrees, stretching our consciousness and unconsciousness out into the virtual world offers us alternative ways of thinking about the extensions of our identities, the nature of the cultural construction of these identities, and the relational dynamics involved in the continual psychological work of identity development in which we participate every day; you could say that part of the role of the SNS is identity testing, an arena where aspects of self are bared within networked publics (boyd, 2008), as discussed in Chapter Four. The way in which one does this will rely a great deal on individual style, but also on upon the generation in which one was born. As Palfrey and Gasser (2008) point out, those of us who happen to be Digital Immigrants (those who did not grow up immersed within digital technology) have had to learn (and continue to learn, sometimes through great resistance) how to "do" digital. Many Digital Immigrants have taken to expressing themselves digitally with ease; for others, online engagement is an alienating and sometimes frightening experience because it runs contrary to received wisdom about notions of intimacy, privacy, and exposure. However, it cannot be emphasised enough that, as a rule, this is not how Digital Natives feel about it. This can be particularly difficult for their parents who misunderstand the online world, and frequently young people wish to keep it that way (Clarke, 2009, p. 74). Those who are Digital Natives know only the digital world in which they were born, a world in which they spend a great deal of their time online:

> Instead of thinking of their digital identity and their real-space identity as separate things, they just have an identity (with representations in two, or three, or more different spaces) . . . For these young people, new digital technologies . . . are primary mediators of human-to-human connections. They have created a 24/7 network that blends the human with the technical to a degree we haven't experienced before, and it is transforming human relationships in fundamental ways. They feel as comfortable in online spaces as they do in offline ones. They don't think of their hybrid lives as anything remarkable. Digital Natives haven't known anything but a life connected to one another, and to the world of bits, in this manner. (Palfrey & Gasser, 2008, pp. 4–5)

While I do not expect that it is wholly true that the distinction between online and offline life is totally blended, it is necessary to highlight that Digital Immigrants are likely to be making distinctions between online and offline life that Digital Natives are not. Furthermore, the fears that children or young people are navigating a scary online world on their own are also unfounded. Clarke's (2009) research indicates that such engagements are subjected to a "group effect", where "online exchanges were mostly either done in the company of friends or reported in full to friends through the online dialogue on their SNSs" (p. 78). Again, we find that online activity, at least as expressed over SNSs, is relational rather than isolated in nature.

It is necessary to be mindful that, in important ways, the way in which individuals manage both the different aspects of their identities and their relationships across digital technologies is not so different from how we understand the nature of the self as being multiply expressed in a variety of different situations, calling upon the mechanism of the false self, or the persona, or, indeed, any of a vast selection of self-states that can be activated at any given time. The nature of our extension into the online world adds another level of subjective experience that allows for potential alienation as well as connection. One cannot assume that an activity is essentially alienating or connecting across an SNS without asking the individual doing the engaging about their experience of it.

Clarke (2009) sees opportunity in online expression, as it offers different developmental opportunities for children and young people dependent upon the developmental needs and potentials that are active for the given individual:

> The fickle way children change their online SNSs and their profiles is similar to the way an adolescent might change his/her appearance. Online, many children appear to adopt a persona that they acknowledge is not necessarily a true reflection of their sense of self but nevertheless is fun to play with, they are aware of themselves changing. (p. 75)

From this perspective, online expressions occur within a transitional space (as described in Chapter Three) in which broad identity exploration can occur: a quasi-magical space to try things on and see what fits. Turkle (2004) similarly agrees:

The online exercise of playing with identity and trying out new ones is perhaps most explicit in role-playing virtual communities and online gaming, where participation literally begins with the creation of a persona or several, but it is by no means confined to these somewhat exotic locales. In bulletin boards, newsgroups, and chat rooms, the creation of personae may be less explicit than in virtual worlds or games, *but it is no less psychologically real*. (p. 21)

The distinction between the rather more fantastical and creative representations of self as experienced in gaming and role playing and those more prosaic uses of persona through SNSs is an important one. The opportunities that these different spaces offer for self-discovery are different, but the *experience of being psychologically real* is similar. The space of psychological reality is similar to what was discussed in the previous chapter with regard to intersubjective space expressed either on or offline being *psychologically real* either way.

The vast majority of users know the difference between what it means to create an imaginative avatar or try out a different persona that is somehow an expression of an otherwise under-expressed aspect of an authentic multiple self. Although some might become addictively caught up in certain expressions of themselves that might provide a defence against problematic or painful self-states, most individuals are distinguishing what is real and what is fantasy. Observers and opinion-makers on the state of social media today, however, are not always so clear about what it is they are criticising. Much of the fear about the online world seems to conflate anxieties into "the Web", "the Internet", or "social media" without expressing precisely which element of virtuality is feared. While it is clear that the ease of access to pornography (especially for young people) is a particular and valid fear that needs addressing (Woods, 2013), this is different from generalised anxiety reactions about "The Internet" in general. Like the space in between any relationship, SNSs can a be place where those multiple and perhaps conflicting aspects of self can be worked through:

For some people, cyberspace is a place to act out unresolved conflicts, to play and replay characterological difficulties on a new and exotic stage. For others, it provides an opportunity to work through significant personal issues, to use the new materials of cybersociality to reach for new resolutions. (Turkle, 2004, p. 22)

The fears that cyber identities are in some way unhinged from reality are generally unfounded in the general population. Identities that are worked through by young people online are created and practised in relation to real social networks (offline and online). boyd (2007) notes that while young people's online identities

> may or may not resemble their offline identity, their primary audience consists of peers that they know primarily offline . . . Because of this direct link between offline and online identities, teens are inclined to present the side of themselves that they believe will be well received by their peers. (p. 13)

Online identity formation can be a way in which young people thoughtfully engage in the possibilities available to them. Frosh (2010), a theorist in psychoanalysis and identity, states that "A central task in life is to find an identity within which one can live, which organises one's experience and allows one to become a 'person'. Identity is *agentic* when thought this way" (p. 100). The notion of an "agentic" identity is an important one, as it reminds us that although identities are responsive to a whole variety of influences in relation to the dynamics of power, with regard to culture, class, capital, and a variety of other things, they are also enacted by individuals making choices in the face of these things. As some parts of our identity are more fixed than others, the space for online play and experimentation may very well be a rather useful way to find oneself in the complex schema of culture and society (on and offline); there is no better way to do this than in relation to others who can respond to the identities that are being tried out: the playback is relational, not digital. The particular nature of fixed and fluid aspects of identity are amenable to a psychodynamic perspective which can give us the tools that we need to gain some purchase on the unconscious functions and mechanisms that are present in the development of identities, "These include the tension between an understanding of identity as something fixed (developmental histories producing stable ways of being that are resistant to change) and indentities as fluid and multiple (unconscious ideas are variable, contradictory and partial)" (Frosh, 2010, p. 101). Not all theorists, however, feel confident that the online arena offers the safest conditions in which to try out identities.

Some psychoanalytic thinkers are responding to the potential challenges to identity in rather hyperbolic ways. Sand (2007), for example, fears that "Society and relational structures are being redefined by cyberspace. Multiple identities can be acted out simultaneously, as one can play as many roles as the number of windows that can fit on one's computer screen" (p. 84). There is a clear "technological determinism" in her words here, seeing "cyberspace" as something that is being "done to" people. Society is not being rewired by cyberspace, rather, as discussed in Chapter Three, society is implicated in the very development of it through social shaping. In any case, the ways in which cyberspace is influencing society is most certainly not the way that Sand suggests. Even though the capability of multiple windows/ multiple roles is indeed possible, we see very little, if any, evidence that individuals are using the possibilities that "cyberspace" offers in this way; the idea that simply because somebody *can* set up scores of online identities because the technology allows it in no way correlates to the fact that this is how people are utilising it. Sand goes on to describe what she terms "interactive identities", which are

> consciously constructed and launched into cyberspace; these identities can be shaped to allow any fantasied aspect of the self to come alive. The interactive self reflects the relationship of the individual to cyberspace, how one uses e-mail, the Internet and multi-user domains . . . (p. 85)

This statement is problematic in a number of ways. First of all, the term "interactive identity" is itself misleading, because all identities are interactive: the matter of identities being different because this interactivity occurs online, as we will see, is a red herring. Although Sand is defining her terms with regard to a *principle of online interactivity*, the term is also problematic due to its lack of precision; she notes that the term is applicable across cyberspace, email, the Internet, and "multi-user domains". Defining "interactive identity" in relation to *online engagement as a category* shifts the focus to the mode of media and away from the psychodynamics of identity deployment themselves: whether the deployment is occurring online or not is simply not the primary issue. Rather, the dynamic that benefits from further exploration is the nature of how an individual deploys their identity in any given interaction (online or not): it is a matter of *that particular deployment for that particular individual, not a matter of it being virtual or face-to-face.*

A notable example of this is how an individual operationalises identity through the medium of an email (one of Sand's examples). There is little fundamental difference between how this process occurs over email, as a general rule, in comparison to how one deploys an identity in a written letter, which they may choose to construct as something that is formal or informal, professional or personal, soppy or dry. The fundamental distinction between an email and a letter is not so much that it is online, it is that the technology lends an email more speed and convenience than a letter, ultimately offering a more direct and instant communication from the sender to the receiver. In fact, one could say that email is rather more amenable to authentic self-expression because it can be sent instantaneously, more often than not revealing an aspect of the self that, in another medium, such as the written letter, would have been suppressed by the superego in the name of social compliance (the very essence of the shame of that email sent too soon). In fact, this function of online immediacy, whether through the sending of an email, the tweeting of a tweet, the updating of a status, or the sending of a text message, paradoxically has the capacity to evade false-self relating simply by way of the sheer ease and speed of such communications. There are a variety of online experiences that avail themselves to instantaneous expressions that have consequences for intersubjectivity that seem to be more a point of interest than the fact that they occur in "cyberspace".

Sand's error of conflating a whole variety of ways in which one might interact in online environments into "interactive identity" in the name of bringing online interaction under the rubric of an object of psychoanalytic study is a common one. This is an error that occludes the lens by pulling focus towards the object of Internet interaction as something fundamentally different from interaction itself. To say such a thing is equivalent to coming to a conclusion about the interactive identity one might possess when "being out in public", This can be demonstrated simply by changing a few words (in italics) in Sand's statement as follows: "The interactive *public* self reflects the relationship of the individual to *public spaces*, how one uses *the underground, the shopping mall and professional and personal* domains". While we should acknowledge that, in some ways, the virtual world offers a different category of experience than the public domain, we also need to bear in mind that *different actions* across the online world also offer fundamentally different expressions of identity and self within that context (e.g., taking on the identity of an other in a networked fantasy game, or interacting with known others on an SNS); simply because one is doing the interacting through the interface of a computer terminal or smartphone does not make these interactions homogeneous. Online spaces are at least as heterogeneous as public spaces can be, if not more so. The most important difference with regard to identity play and other activities online and identity play and other activities offline is neither the danger of losing touch with reality nor identifying fully with an avatar self. The fundamental differences between identity play online and real life fall into four broad categories of online difference:

1. The instantaneous nature of online engagements.
2. The ease of replicability of information online (enhanced by point one).
3. The ease with which privacy can be lost (enhanced by points one and two).
4. The way in which information logged online may never be erased and may be accessed at any time (synergises with points one, two, and three).

These categories work synergistically, with each one creating an enhanced effect for the rest of them. These four categories resonate closely with the properties that boyd (2008) associates with networked publics, principles which include "replicability and "persistence [of data]" alongside additional features of "scalablity", in which "the potential visibility of content in networked publics is great", and "searchability" (p. 27). Both my categories of online difference and boyd's (2008) properties of networked publics importantly include the presence of a "digital dossier" (Palfrey & Gasser, 2008), which is the collection of all the information available on the Internet and locatable to a single human being, generally available to search engines such as Google, and, even more recently, Facebook. This information may be passively collated across a search engine such as Google (as described in Chapter Two), which we can call an "passive digital dossier", though more and more individuals are actively creating their own through their histories on SNSs (applications like Social Me can display the major points of a digital dossier in about a minute and half), which we can call an "active digital dossier". Because Digital

Natives have come into being after the advent of Web 2.0, the conse-quences of having a digital dossier are different for them than their elders, as their dossiers go back further and will ultimately contain a great deal more information within them.

Children and young people: ease, replicability, privacy, and the digital dossier

The starting age for the use of social networks is getting earlier, des-pite the minimum age restrictions of some platforms (Clarke, 2009). A consequence of the digital divide between Natives and Immigrants is that teachers and parents are unfamiliar with the digital worlds of their children, resulting in many parents reporting that their children know more about the Internet than they do (Clarke, 2009, p. 57). Therefore, when parents bar their children from using SNSs, children are frequently quite forgiving because they see their parents as being misguided about online life, "For instance, many children made the clear distinction between social networking sites—which have privacy settings—and chat rooms which are open to anyone". These are distinctions that parents are less likely to make (Clarke, 2009, p. 60), not to mention psychoanalysts and social theorists (see above). For these reasons and others, adults tend to be more circumspect when it comes to what they might share or not on a social network, while chil-dren and young people are less so. In the light of the categories of difference mentioned above (instantaneousness, replicability, loss of privacy, and the digital dossier), it is fair to say that the consequences of identity expression online may have different consequences for younger people that it does for Digital Immigrants. The instantaneous nature of digital presence enables a more immediate (sometimes unthought through) posting of material on the Internet that can be immediately replicated as soon as it is posted (even if it is removed shortly after). This replication means that the privacy of an individual, who might have believed that they were posting on a trusted network (e.g., among known Facebook friends), finds that this privacy has been breached (as commonly happens in cyberbullying). These post-ings, whether they are regrettable breaches or not, remain attached to the user's profile, potentially following them through life on their digital dossier. O'Keefe and Clarke-Pearson (2011), who prefer the term "digital footprint", warn of the consequences of the way in which it builds cumulatively across a lifetime:

> Preadoescents [sic] and adolescents who lack an awareness of privacy issues often post inappropriate messages, pictures, and videos . . . without the concomitant understanding that what they are posting online is likely to remain there. (O'Keefe & Clarke-Pearson, 2011, p. 802)

While O'Keefe and Clarke-Pearson go on to discuss the consequences of this for university admissions or future employment, I would argue that the bigger issue is a psychodynamic one rather than the logistical one. Because we have an entire generation growing up in the same boat, I predict that future employers and university admissions officers will be more forgiving of digital dossiers in the future; after all, those employers and admissions officers will have digital dossiers, themselves. However, the way in which a digital dossier that is difficult to drop will affect identity development in young people is a different question all together.

An example of one of the substantive changes between Digital Immigrants and Natives is the portability of an active digital dossier via SNSs. One of the great possibilities available to Digital Immigrants in their youth (retrospectively viewed as a freedom) was that when one changed schools, locations, or moved on to university or on to work, many were able, at least to some to degree, to start from scratch. However, if a Digital Native is carrying around an SNS profile from one stage of their life to the next, how will they have the chance to experience such a freedom? Turkle (2011) notes, rather succinctly, that "it is not so easy to experiment when all rehearsals are archived" (p. 273). Palfrey and Gasser (2008) use the metaphor of the digital dossier in relation to Digital Natives as being like a tattoo, "something connected to them that they cannot get rid of later in life, even if they want to, without a great deal of difficulty" (p. 53). Palfrey and Gasser go on to describe the nature of Digital Native identities as a double paradox. The first paradox is that although today's digital identities "can be adjusted with ease", the ability to control how an identity is perceived by others is "far less under our control—than ever before" (p. 34). The second paradox operates on the premise that real-life identities (like the persona) can be tailored for the different environments for which they are required, and these aspects of self are, to some degree, compartmentalised in different contexts (an individual as a student, as a daughter, at an after-school job, as a best friend). "The paradox arises" online, according to Palfrey and Gasser (2009),

> because from the perspective of the onlooker, much more of the Digital Native's identity may be visible at any one moment than was possible for individuals in pre-Internet eras. If the Digital Native has created multiple identities, those identities might be connected to create a much fuller picture of the individual than was possible before, spanning a greater period of time. (p. 35)

This situation is exactly what makes the SNS so uncomfortable in managing a combination of close friends, work colleagues, and family all in one virtual place. While there are similar consequences for Digital Immigrants, the embedded nature of the Digital Native in their online world has a deeper effect, as the object relations point of view tells us with regard to the process of identification.

As we learnt in the previous chapter, in the psychodynamic process of identification, the object (which is the mental representation of the other) is brought inside the psyche itself. For Freud (1923b) the ego itself is made from the accretion of such object identifications, "the character of the ego is a precipitate of abandoned object cathexes and . . . contains the history of those object cathexes" (p. 29). As this theory was developed by intersubjectivity and relational psychoanalysis, we came to see how the gaze of the other is also fundamental in the development of the self in identification. As Aron (1996) points out, the paradigm shift of the relational approach is that the study of the mind has moved from seeing it as existing "independently and autonomously within the boundaries of the individual [as in the classical stance] to the relational notion that mind is inherently dyadic, social, interactional and interpersonal" (p. x). Hence, the development of identity comes back to the concept of mutual recognition and the interactional mutual co-construction of identity as a dyadic (at least) process. SNSs are, no doubt, interactional platforms; this is, in fact, their *raison d'être*. It is for these reasons that authors such as boyd (2007), Clarke (2009), and Turkle (2011) see so much potential in identity play over them. However, when compared to the kind of transitional magical play discussed in Chapter Five, there is a major difference: the concretisation of the play. Transitional space between subjects in the real world is an evanescent affair, the psyche takes and receives and develops in a fluid-like trajectory from one experience to the next. It is quite possible that transitional play across an SNS works in analogous ways—however, the digital recording of such play is bound to have its consequences.

The presence of the digital dossier produces a continued paradox when examined through the lens of intrapsychic and intersubjective experience of identity within the individual and between individuals. Consider the components of a full (active and passive) digital dossier: passive fragments about the self as collected through a search engine such as Google, active fragments about the self as collected through *other* people's use of a social network (e.g., photos of the individual posted on a friend's SNS, comments that tag this individual, etc.), and constellations of information about a self composed on one's own social network profile. All of these fragments will contain, to a greater or lesser degree, emotional investments (cathexes) of that individual (e.g., a photograph from a particularly fulfilling or difficult time in one's life; a comment on a wall from a lost individual). In the previous chapter, we discussed the model of Freud's (1917e) "Mourning and melancholia", in which the way one deals with their investment (cathexis) with the object will determine whether or not they experience mourning or melancholia. It is worth reminding ourselves of Freud's quote from the previous chapter with regard to the implicit expansion of what an object can be: "every single one of the memories and expectations in which the libido is bound to the object is brought up and hyper-cathected" (1917e, p. 245). In other words, in order to let go of an object, in order to mourn it, each part (memory and expectation) has to be let go of with an accompanying release of energy. What if these memories and expectations are preserved, as they are in many ways within a digital dossier? The presence of these cathected objects as they remain online have the capacity to "haunt" an individual simply due to their ineradicable presence and their capacity to be revisited again and again. No doubt, long ago, the technology that allowed the arrival of family photographs into the homes of the general public had a similar effect on the response to the death of a loved one. Never before were most individuals (those who did not have access to painted portraits) able to see the faces of their loved ones again. The idea of emoting while looking at an old photo album or a box full of snaps is now a cliché, but it was not always so. The presence of not only photographs, but also comments, thoughts, and entire conversations online bring this phenomenon to a whole new level. The functioning of the ever-presence of the digital dossier is reminiscent of one of Freud's minor, but rather whimsical, papers entitled "A note on the 'mystic writing pad'". In this paper, Freud describes a piece of simple technology of his time as a metaphor for how the perceptual system of the mind may operate with regard to what is conscious (that is, what is available in the mind right now, like these words you are reading) and what is preconscious (that is, anything below consciousness that is not repressed, such as memories). Freud (1925a) states that "the perceptual apparatus of our mind consists of two layers, of an external protective shield against stimuli whose task it is to diminish the strength of excitations coming in, and the surface behind it which receives the stimuli" (p. 230). The mystic writing pad is a device that similarly has two layers: one piece of thin waxed paper that lay atop a wax tablet. One can write on this paper with a stylus, but once the paper is lifted from the wax tablet, the writing disappears and it can be written up fresh another time:

> The surface of the Mystic Pad is clear of writing and once more capable of receiving impressions. But it is easy to discover that the permanent trace of what was written is retained upon the wax slab itself and is legible in suitable lights. The Pad provides not only a receptive surface that can be used over and over again, like a slate, but also permanent traces of what has been written . . . it solves the problem of combining the two functions *by dividing them between two separate but interrelated component parts or systems* . . . The layer which receives the stimuli . . . forms no permanent traces; the foundations of memory come about in other, adjoining systems. (Freud, 1925a, p. 230)

On an SNS, these two functions are combined into one; that which is written is retained forever, one simply has to scroll down to see it. In this case, a life on social media no longer exists in the waxy indeterminate world of the pre-conscious as described by Freud, above, but, rather, in an open and visible public consciousness always available to view by one's self or anybody else who has access to it. The consequences for the ever-presence of a digital dossier offer new challenges to identity; these challenges are very now, very contemporary, but not "postmodern".

Call it the contemporary state of things
but please don't call it postmodern

The sheer possibilities offered by the online digital world in all its capacities appears to be an open invitation for cultural theorists to apply much loved discourses to it, often presenting the possibilities that it offers as evidence of the postmodern world view. "Postmodern" is a notoriously difficult concept, and, in many ways, the term reflects the body of theory, which is rather difficult to pin down. Although the term arose in particular reference to Lyotard's (1984) text, *The Postmodern Condition: A Report on Knowledge*, it has come to represent a whole body of theory that aims to de-centre the idea of objective knowledge; it is very popular in the discipline of identity politics. I use it here in its widest sense, as I have defined it previously (Balick, 2011b) by contrasting it to rational modernism, which sought to apply objective knowledge to "previously undiscovered domains of experience" (p. 17). Loewenthal and Snell (2003) take a rather lyrical perspective to postmodernism (a common postmodern style), noting that postmodern thinking prefers

> Diversity, multiplicity, and uncertainty, over system, ideology and generalisation; play decoration and idiosyncrasy, over coherence and transparency; irony and questioning, over received wisdom or established authority ... It would question the supremacy of reason and consciousness, offering instead a 'decentred' vision of what it is to be human. (p. 5)

Postmodernism seeks to challenge the entire epistemology of the modern rational view, preferring a more multiple, relativist, and deconstructive approach to knowledge and "truth", which is seen to be both socially constructed, contingent, and fully embedded in cultural power mechanisms. Postmodernism has a particular interest in identity, which it sees as being

> neither essential nor solid: rather it is something that is created within a social context, and hence comes along with all the social values and inherent epistemic power mechanisms as a result of this construction. Furthermore, the specifying and disciplining nature of identities has taken the foreground, resulting in a general suspicion of identity categories: this is an inheritance that can be traced back to Foucault. (Balick, 2011b, p. 17)

In considering these preferences of the postmodern position, one can see why, given the multiple possibilities that the online world offers with regard to the open and decentralised way in which it operates, the infinite ways in which it distributes and replicates information, and the ease with which one can express oneself in multiple ways, cyberspace seems to offer an open invitation to postmodern theorising.

While I concur that a postmodern perspective may indeed offer some important insights, a postmodern "open season" on the ways that identities are perceived to be expressed online would not be a helpful approach. Establishing what he sees as the difficulty in the postmodern project on the whole, Frosh (2006) draws a distinction between the possible uses of postmodern thinking while, at the same time, addressing its formal difficulties:

> [D]espite the deep seriousness of the postmodernist project, its intellectualism and tendency to mesh deconstructionism with autocritique has sometimes made it seem cynical and anarchic, as if it had no values at all . . . this is a *misrepresentation* of the postmodern position, but it is nevertheless *symptomatic* of the postmodernism condition, in which meaning is sacrificed in the name of style. (p. 370, my italics)

Frosh's distinction here is an important one, because it shows that the thoughtful application of the insights of many postmodern theorists can offer us a great deal, but only if deployed with care and precision. Seidman (1993), though postmodern in many of his perspectives, none the less has argued that not all cohesive identities are limiting, "Identity constructions are not disciplining and regulatory only in self-limiting and oppressive ways; they are also personally, socially and politically enabling" (p. 134). Although Seidman is speaking particularly about sexual identities here, the axis between whether an identity is liberating or constricting operates across all identity constructions including class, gender, race, etc.; a construction can be liberating or constricting, whether it is fluid or stable. In my own previous research (Balick, 2008, 2011b), I have found that often, when a postmodern perspective is applied to clinical work, particularly in relation to identity, the position can operate as an ideology that impels clinicians in unhelpful ways due to an implicit political imperative to deconstruct stable identities. Despite the fact that the postmodern project was created in the name of a subversive liberation of identity from its embeddedness in social power structures, Frosh (2006) notes that "even the assumption that democratising and narrativising the therapeutic situation is necessarily good is in itself, unavoidably, an imposition of a certain mode of therapeutic ideology" (p. 376). Here, Frosh is noting that the direct implementation of postmodern ideology into clinical practice is no guarantee of freeing such practice from ideology. As I see it, in this case, the paradigm of a stable identity is seen, by postmodern clinical practice, as less developed than the fluid identities that such an ideology celebrates and espouses. In this case, the implicit ideological position of multiplicity, deconstruction, and fluidity .

> continues a notion of 'therapist knows best' whereby the most 'accomplished' and developed position is [identity] fluidity . . . a balance needs to be struck here, a balance in which the postmodern notion of unstable identities is engaged with, while a the same time not used as a monolithic approach. (Balick, 2011b, p. 22)

A monolithic approach results in a fetishisation of the fluid identity, whereas a balanced approach allows insight into the decentred aspects of identity without requiring it to be something more than that. Although identities are *enacted or deployed* in a variety of different ways, they ultimately reside within a general constellation of subjective experience (however multiple or "fluid") that is generally somewhat cohesive; in fact, most people experience distress when identity cohesion becomes compromised. Turkle (2004) notes that, despite postmodern discourse, which argues strongly against unitary expressions of self in favour of identities that are multiple, fluid, and decentred: "the normal requirements of everyday life exert strong pressure on people to take responsibility for their actions and to see themselves as unitary actors" (p. 24). The playground of the online world, however, can enable an expression of this postmodern multiplicity, perhaps, in some cases, as a break from the requirements of being a cohesive self in real life. Still, as I have been pointing towards throughout this text, we have to examine the multiple ways in which individuals are interacting, phenomenologically, with others in their online worlds. As we have seen, most people's use, across SNSs at least, are generally close enough representations of an individual's real representation of themselves. Should an individual choose to go on to an SNS with an altered identity, this is a choice they are making that will be based on some psychodynamic motivation, perhaps to have an aspect of themselves witnessed that gets very little attention through conventional channels; in this case, what is being put into the foreground may be a shadowed aspect of the real self. Turkle (2004) notes that cyberspace can be "an object *to think with* for thinking about identity" (p. 24: my italics). This idea of the online world being something to "think with" is an interesting one and reflects on the myriad ways in which virtuality mediates not just interrelations between people, but also between aspects of the self; it becomes a playground not just to explore transitional space, as discussed in Chapter Five, but also the internal space of an individual's identity. Constructing cyberspace as a tool that one might use to think about their identity allows one to pull the focus away from the postmodern imperative to see it only as an expression of fluidity. Rather, cyberspace allows meaning to be made of multiple aspects of self, instead of simply an expression of a decentred, deconstructed, postmodern identity. Turkle (2004) goes on to describe it like this:

> Once we have literally written our online personae into existence, they can be a kind of Rorschach. We can use them to become more aware of what we are projecting into everyday life. We can use the virtual to reflect the real. Cyberspace opens the possibility for identity play, but it is very serious play. People who cultivate an awareness of what stands behind their screen personae are the ones most likely to succeed in using virtual experience for personal and social transformation. And the people who make the most of their lives on the screen are those who are capable of approaching it in a spirit of self reflection. (p. 22)

When online identity play is used in this way, it offers up an opportunity, in fact, to come closer to understanding a self that, though multiple in its expression, is also cohesive as a particular unique and idiosyncratic constellation of parts.

Alternatively, Sand (2007) prefers the language of postmodernity in talking about what she calls ideational space:

> This ideational space is created by the mind, dependent on language and often projected onto a fantasied other. The narrative text is performative, becoming the medium through which different aspects of identity and the self are constructed and conveyed. Cyberspace can be

both an ideational and transitional space as identities are created to fill multiple conscious and unconscious needs. (pp. 85–86)

Most of the time, life online is simply much more prosaic than this, which may explain the success of Facebook, in which representations of the self are close to both self-perception and the perceptions of others (Back et al., 2011; boyd, 2007), and the relative demise of Second Life, in which fantasy avatars are used in a virtual landscape that is, in so many ways, unhinged from our real world. The problem in applying postmodern perspectives to cyberspace is not so much that they are *wrong*, but that, as described above, "cyberspace" is not a unitary construct. While "cyberspace" as an interesting concept as a whole seems very attractive to postmodern theorising, we find that the meanings that individuals make of their experiences are bound in those *experiences themselves* across a myriad of cyberspace locations that can be operationalised in a variety of different ways. In this case, the psychodynamic approach is apt because it makes itself available to understand interaction, relating, meaning-making, and unconscious motivations; it endeavours to look at the process of individuals engaged in the *relating aspects* of their online experiences rather than the "being online" itself. This is an inheritance from the clinic, where analytic boundaries and creating a safe space is paramount to enable an individual to explore their identity (in all its modes of experience) and their unconscious relational structures. In relation to this paradigm received from the clinical perspective, Gibbs (2007) feels that a reliance on postmodern conceptions of relative or constructed realities is actually dangerous:

I have found that postmodern concepts that insist that there is no actual, objective reality have limitations in terms of their application to analytic technique. A consideration of virtual reality, and of reality within the 'as if' nature of the transference, must be done with an appreciation of the analyst's authoritative role in analyzing and providing boundaries through the vehicle of interpretive technique. Clinical techniques based upon epistemological premises that there is no reality, or that we cannot know what reality is, are in my experience, misguided and can have quite deleterious clinical outcomes. (p. 17)

One of the great difficulties of postmodern perspectives in the past was that they were epistemologies that were developed outside the clinical situation developed with no intention of becoming part of the clinical encounter. Their insights, none the less, have found their way into psychoanalysis, mostly in ways that have been positive to the development of theory and practice. Particularly with regard to relational theory, this has been a boon because it has, in reality, democratised the therapeutic process into one in which it is now explicit that there are multiple points of view present, and that the experiences that occur in the consultation room are mutually co-constructed. This is a balance between Gibb's fear, voiced above, that there is "no reality", and the old-fashioned stance that analyst authority is the only authority that has any "objective" insight. These insights are extrapolated here to show that online interaction with others can be used as a tool with which to think about identity. Selfhood is a continual, interactive, and co-constructed event that occurs between real people and is more and more mediated online. Relational meaning is derived from online and offline intersubjective experiences. A variety of theoretical perspectives can be brought to bear on these phenomena to better understand them, and a multi-disciplinary approach will make the findings richer all around. However, these perspectives and approaches will give us insight into online relating so long as they keep in mind two important provisos; that there must be precision in the nature of the online relating that is being investigated (i.e., not on "cyberspace" as a whole, but what kind of function is being mediated by it and how) and that any ideologies brought to bear upon it are recognised, declared, and handled with care.

Conclusion

"There are known knowns; there are things we know we know.
We also know there are known unknowns; that is to say, we
know there are some things we do not know. But there are also
unknown unknowns—the ones we don't know we don't know"

(Donald Rumsfeld, United States Secretary of Defense, 2002)

In the introduction to this book, I noted that I wished to do all that I
could to "future proof" it so that it could stand up to the rapidly
changing nature of our online social networking world. As I
readied the manuscript for submission, I found myself inundated with
news stories surrounding the psychological and emotional consequences of online social networking within our culture that I felt I
needed to incorporate into the text. For example, in the weeks before
submission, the *Question Time* trolling story broke in relation to Mary
Beard, and has now been included in Chapter Four; within a week of
that I was made aware of the cyberstalking case of James Lasdun
through an article in the *Guardian Weekend Magazine* (Lasdun, 2013a),
which I then incorporated into Chapter Two; and this very week
(August, 2013) as I place my final comments on the galley proofs of
this very book, the press is awash with news of and comments on the

shocking threats delivered to Caroline Criado-Perez over Twitter in response to her campaign to get Jane Austen onto the ten pound note. In addition to personal interest stories, important research was released in the weeks before submission as well, including the *Future Identities* report conducted by the UK Government Office for Science (Foresight Future Identities, 2013) and several *Pew Internet and American Life* Reports including "The demographics of social media users—2012" (Duggan & Brenner, 2013), and "Coming and going on Facebook" (Rainie, Smith, & Duggan, 2013). Fortunately, one of the great boons of today's Internet is that all of these reports are freely available online, and can be accessed simply by visiting the websites listed in the references section of this book.[31] Alas, the manuscript had to be submitted, and I am sure that by the time it goes to press there will have been scores, if not hundreds, of other examples emerging in the press that resonate with the findings of this text. While it is my hope that the dynamics I have outlined within will be applicable to further stories and research as they emerge after the publication of this book, there will no doubt be enough material in the coming years for further updated editions. In the meantime, this conclusion will reflect on some of the latest data relevant to what I have already covered in the text, and then move on to some general concluding thoughts and recommendations.

The structure of this book was intended to work though a series of dynamics, contexts, and angles that culminated in a final chapter on identities, which are intrinsically related to selfhood. Selfhood may be seen as "the potential for integration of the total personality" (Samuels, 1985, p. 91). Since identities are fundamentally relational in nature, it is only by laying down the relational groundwork first that we could come to understand how our connected-up instantaneous culture affects the complex nature of our selfhoods as they become more and more mediated online. The recent *Future Identities* report resonates with the themes of the previous chapter by concluding that, "the internet has not produced a new kind of identity. Rather it has been instrumental in raising awareness that identities are more multiple, culturally contingent and contextual than had previously been understood" (Foresight Future Identities, 2013, p. 1). That the authors use the term "raising awareness" indicates that it is not the identities themselves that have changed, but, rather, the ways in which culture is perceiving them that is shifting. This awareness is driven by what the authors' term "hyper-connectivity", which they define as:

the use of multiple communications systems and devices to remain constantly connected to social networks and streams of information. Hyper-connectivity has several key attributes: being 'always on' . . . readily accessible; information-rich beyond any individual's capacity to consume; interactive, not only between people but also involving people-to-machine and machine-to-machine communications; and always recording, with virtually unlimited storage capacity facilitating peoples' desire to document their lives. (p. 29)

This is, indeed, the environment that I described in Chapter Three and termed "The matrix". The authors of this report go on to recognise the value of identities as activated within this matrix on a number of different levels, including personal, psychological, social, and commercial. They note that identities are inclusive of both self-perceptions and the perceptions of others, that they contain overlapping categories such as "ethnic, religious, national, age, family, financial, online" (p. 3), and that people express their identities in different ways. Like Valenzuela, Park, and Kee (2009) these authors understand that identities have social capital. People are utilising SNSs to engage on all of these levels in a multiplicity of ways, and younger people, as a rule, are deploying themselves across SNSs more readily than older people. The latest numbers from the USA indicate that sixty-seven per cent of Internet users use Facebook, sixteen per cent use Twitter, fifteen per cent use Pinterest, thirteen per cent Instagram, and six per cent Tumblr;[32] eighty-three per cent of those in the age group of 18–25 are likely to use a social networking site of any kind (Duggan & Brenner, 2013, p. 2). While the "digital divide" used to refer to those who had Internet access and those who did not, it can now be seen to be more generational, with the younger generation being more connected-up than ever, deploying much of their identities, relationships, and social capital across online social networks.

These numbers, particularly in relation to the generational divide, seem to indicate that there is no going back; identity, social life and relationships are now mediated online as a *primary location* for those under twenty-five as a rule, but a sizable and growing proportion of those who are older as well. However, there are some rumblings that there may be a backlash of sorts. Research by Rainie, Smith, and Duggan (2013) notes that sixty-one per cent of Facebook users have voluntarily taken a break from it for several weeks or more, and a full twenty per cent of online adults who have once been on Facebook are no longer using it; only eight per cent of adults currently not on Facebook wish to become a user (p. 1). Anecdotally, some children are losing interest in Facebook simply because their parents are on it (Van Grove, 2013); they are moving to Twitter or other SNSs not yet colonised by their parent's generation. While nearly seventy per cent of the research subjects estimated they would spend the same amount of time on Facebook next year as they do this year, twenty-seven per cent plan to spend less time on it, with a tiny three per cent wishing to spend more time (Van Grove, 2013, p. 1). How these numbers will pan out, and how users will come to understand how fulfilling or not their Facebook use is, is not yet known. The psychodynamics of instantaneous, connected-up culture has its consequences, and one of the consequences of hyper-connectivity may be a kind of relational fatigue, a fatigue that is further exacerbated by the lack of boundaries present in the online world. Hartman (2011) puts the lack of boundaries in cyberspace in perspective by contrasting them to the way in which maintaining boundaries is seen to be so important to the psychoanalytic setting:

> By comparison to our historical, psychoanalytic emphasis on a boundaried reality that can be modified by fantasy to mediate inevitable loss, the new cyber reality is limitless. Not circumscribed by 'potential space' that articulates the subject in deference to the environment, it has the expansiveness of infinite space. Not constrained by consensus, it is a reality that need simply be declared. I present myself, therefore I am: I give access to myself therefore I relate. I am right there on Facebook. Come find me. I was lost; now I'm found. (pp. 472–473)

Greif (2011) similarly reflects on the contrasting nature between psychoanalytic space and our contemporary, connected-up world. He notes how the very practice of psychoanalysis or psychoanalytic psychotherapy offers an alternative to instantaneous connect-up culture by drawing a comparative metaphor to the "slow food" movement. The bounded psychoanalytic session offers an individual a chance to slow down, reconnect, come out of being "plugged in", and be with another individual in a profoundly grounded and intimate way.

Boundaries can be wearing, but so can the lack of them. The boundary-less nature of the Internet offers as much as it takes away. Most importantly, it changes the domain of our selfhood because it expands the overall space into which our selfhood can extend and the speed and replicability with which it can meet that expansion. As discussed in Chapter Four, boundary-less space encourages a regressive sense of omnipotence which, when confronted with limit, can ultimately result in feelings of anxiety, depression, and loneliness. In returning to the question asked in the introduction, and then reintroduced in the previous chapter, we wonder again: is the development of what has come to be called "Web 2.0" changing us in some fundamental way, or is it simply a novel technological platform through which the same old psychological traits express themselves through a different medium?

It is tempting to take the psychoanalytic prerogative here and turn the question back on the reader, but that would be a cop-out. In Chapter One, I argued that psychoanalysis is up to the task of answering these sorts of questions; I hope now to have demonstrated that this is the case. Seligman (2011) draws our attention to the "analytic postulate" in which "most anything can stand for anything" and, using psychoanalytic reasoning, looks at what the Internet itself might stand for:

> Particular objects, forms, and media will lend themselves to certain particular uses . . . The Internet and its media carry the contemporary crises of privacy, overstimulation, and the broad questions of where and by whom reality is adjudicated. (p. 502)

Sand (2007) similarly notes that

> We need to expand our analytic boundaries to incorporate these new aspects of self [provoked by the online world], or risk becoming stagnant and outdated as we lose the interactive richness of what will soon be an integral part of all our patients' experience. (p. 87)

Sand is correct in this. While a variety of researchers from diverse backgrounds (e.g., sociology, experimental psychology, marketing, and the computer and behavioural sciences) are producing copious amounts of quantitative and nomothetic data on the effect of online social networking and culture on a rather wide scale, psychodynamic researchers have not been so quick to bring their insights to the table with regard to applied research in this area. Perhaps this is due to a sense, in psychodynamic psychotherapists and researchers, that online social networking is too far removed from the intimacy created in the consulting room. Although in some ways this may be true, I hope that I have shown by way of Chapter Two and other uses of psychodynamic theory throughout this book that psychoanalysis has a valuable functional and conceptual frame to offer this area of enquiry. The current *cybersituation* is one that psychodynamic theoreticians and clinicians can no longer turn their heads from in fear or incomprehension, simply hoping that it will go away. Seligman (2011) puts this fear clearly from the perspective of psychoanalysis:

> By and large, psychoanalysts and their fellow travellers have feared the loss of authenticity and the blurring of the distinction between fantasy and reality, seeing the cyberworld as a diversion from the possibilities of truer human contact, both with others and with the deeper dimensions of the self so crucial to a rich and flexible way of life. For them, electronic social life is a poor substitute for actual connection, consoling perhaps, but unreal nonetheless. (p. 500)

It is time to move away from the "unreal nonetheless" perspective. Holding on to such a perspective diminishes not only the more than a billion people who utilise SNSs in a variety of ways and contexts, but also risks alienating an entire generation for whom SNS relating is psychologically real and a part of everyday life. Asking what is "real" goes back to the foundational principles of psychoanalysis with regard to what Freud called "psychical reality" or "internal reality", defined as "the conviction of the reality of the psychic world that exists unconsciously and is felt as inside the person" (Hinshelwood, 1991, p. 330); psychic reality is what feels real without reference to external reality and was present as an important and fundamental component of relationships long before there was an "online" that demanded someone to arbitrate what was real and what was not. From the object relations perspective, we see the reality that exists between two individual subjects as being replete with phantasy and illusion. Contemporary psychoanalysts work *in the transference* every day, identifying the projections of their patients and "reality testing" them through the interplay that they experience with them in the consulting room. The *unreality* of online relating is no more or no less real than the dynamics that occur in this live, intersubjective space.

In any case, however "unreal" many still claim the relational psychodynamics of online life may be, the real world consequences of online life are not hard to find; just ask Mary Beard, James Lasdun,

Caroline Criado-Perez, or refer back to my own experience in Chapter Two. The question of whether relating virtually is real or not should now be clear; it is real, but it is also different. In Chapter Six, I enumerated four categories that differentiated identity play and other online activity from the same in real life. They included instantaneousness, replicability, risk to privacy, and the digital dossier: each works synergistically with the other. These categories are affecting the reality of everyday relationships between people by way of mediated relating, virtual impingement, transference, projection, etc., but they have particular consequences for different kinds of professional relationships, too. Privacy concerns with regard to social networking are fast becoming a concern to a class of professionals for whom privacy is particularly relevant. Top among them, of course, are psychotherapists, but also medical doctors and other related professionals.

Many professional groupings have been late getting to understand the phenomena and to make policy in response to it. While these responses may be well meaning, they may also suffer from responding to the content nature of online social networking rather than taking a more thoughtful, process-orientated approach. That is, they are not based on the underlying psychodynamics of the material at hand. McCartney (2012), writing in the *British Medical Journal* notes a series of instances in a variety of professions including nursing and the police, where inappropriate Facebook postings resulted in sackings. While it may seem obvious that the sharing of confidential information should be avoided, it does nonetheless happen because police and nurses are people too, and these people as we have seen, are more and more likely to conflate private and public, professional and personal domains through the extensions of themselves online. As McCartney describes, many doctors may find themselves exposing confidential material without intention simply by consulting online with colleagues in the interest of their patients: public access to these discussions not only constitutes a breach of confidentiality, but may, indeed, constitute breaking the law in the form of the Data Protection Act in the UK. Outside these direct infringements of privacy are the more subtle aspects of the online social world: they may not directly contravene them. In these cases, the British Medical Association recommends that medical doctors do not "friend" current or former patients on Facebook. Furthermore, the potential for doctors' online profiles, such as on Facebook, to become public raises the recurring question about whether the way any given doctor behaves in her private life can be held accountable in the professional sphere. McCartney's (2012) conclusion is a sensible but cautious one, recognising that any given doctor cannot be fooled into thinking their online private life is entirely different from their professional life, while at the same time stating that they

> must not be overly cautious and miss the richness of communication and interaction that social media can offer. Doctors, like other citizens, are entitled to express opinions online, and one effect of the undoing of the medical god-complex has been to humanise medicine and populate it with doctors who are fallible but professional. (e440)

This is a rather thoughtful and subtle approach that acknowledges the complexity of online life.

Surprisingly, from within the mental health field, one can find some examples that are not quite so subtle and seem to lack the insights from psychodynamic thinking that one would think would be foundational to the field itself. The tone of Arehart-Treichel's (2011) article "Facebook can be useful – if you use common sense" in *Psychiatric News*, for example, strikes me as rather naïve this late in the Facebook game. It concludes with three bullet points of advice including being aware of privacy settings, not "friending" patients, and controlling what goes on your own personal pages: common sense indeed. Arehart-Treichel cites psychiatrist Raymond Lam, who suggests that psychiatrists simply "ignore" friend requests from clients, and only broach the subject if they bring it up themselves (5A). I find this approach far too passive and completely lacking in the insight and sensitivity we might expect from a field that should be thinking more psychologically about its service users; it also denotes an almost complete incomprehension of the scale and ubiquity of online social life among the general public, and particularly for younger people, who are less likely to be making "boundaried" distinctions when seeking "friends" or contacts across their social networks. A more comprehensive approach, as pioneered by Kolmes, Nagel, and Anthony (2011) and Kolmes (2012), enables a more holistic approach in which fuller questions and themes can be explored in relation to the individual ways in which particular therapists may be working; various registering bodies are creating their own procedural and ethical guidelines for social networking and online relating.

It is important to note in these concluding words that professional organisations are still finding their feet in this rapidly changing world of online relating. While it is vital that institutions and professional organisations create their own codes of ethics and procedures with regard to social networking, it is also incumbent upon them to think psychologically (if not psychodynamically) about the choices they are making in the construction of such codes. This text hopes to have made a start with regard to a conceptual framework to apply to online relating *as an extension of human relating*. It acknowledges that virtual relating is real and that it is different. To return to the original question posed above, I have come to the conclusion that, due to the four categories of instantaneousness, replicability, risk to privacy, and the digital dossier, it is indeed likely that the way in which we are relating online may be changing us in some way—to borrow from Kranzberg (1986), this is neither good nor bad, but neither is it neutral. In order to come to a greater understanding of the consequences of this brave new world of relating, we must expand research into the meanings that individuals are making of their experiences through qualitative phenomenological psychosocial research. Such research can be done in tandem with larger-scale studies to broaden our understanding of this fast developing world. The need to relate has not changed. The need to recognise and be recognised has not changed. The need to seek and be sought has not been altered. The architecture, however, of the ways we do all these fundamental things that make us human has indeed changed, and that may be changing us; for these reasons, we need to understand the psychodynamics of social networking.

NOTES

1. The development of the Internet itself is a very interesting story that goes beyond the scope of this book, but interested readers can find a concise history in Naughton (2012a). In this section, I briefly discuss the development of what might be called the social web, which is only a small part of both the history and the content of the Internet as a whole.
2. The speed of information travelling across a threshold (very slow in these early days).
3. The language of object relations theory is an inheritance of its past, in which other people were seen as the "objects" through with the libido sought its release, and, furthermore, how these objects were introjected (internalised) to become parts of the self. The importance of the external "objects" coming to be perceived as human subjects in their own right required the shift in theory to the relational position.
4. This failure to collect what I wished to over Facebook has been an important lesson in my own learning about how different SNSs lend themselves to different kinds of research purposes. The fact that Facebook is usually attached to a user's real name and personality has an inhibiting effect on individuals' sharing of personal stories on a public Facebook page.
5. Addressing the broader social and political ramifications of the loss of privacy is beyond the scope of this book; however, it is important to bear in mind Naughton's (2012a) insight,

> For governments of all political stripes – from authoritarian regimes to liberal democracies – the Internet is a surveillance tool made in heaven, because much of the surveillance can be done, not by expensive and fallibly human beings, but by computers. (p. 163)

6. Even here we find exceptions, particularly in religious ceremonies, where we find intentional starvation (fasting) as in Ramadan and Yom Kippur, and traditional bingeing as in Christmas or Thanksgiving.
7. For those interested in a more comprehensive history of the development of object relations and relational theory, see Greenberg and Mitchell (1983).
8. This is where the idea of a neutral analyst as "blank screen" comes from. By remaining neutral, the analyst maintains her role as "object" to invite uncontaminated transferences that can than be interpreted. The idea of neutrality and the "blank screen" has been largely dispensed with today by all manner of psychoanalysts, though many employ versions of it according to their training.
9. Winnicott sometimes capitalises "true self" and "false self" and sometimes he does not. I have chosen to keep them in lower case, but have retained the capitalisations from the original text. Jung does not capitalise persona.
10. The phrase "primary care-giver" is more appropriate, as it describes any individual who might be an infant's first and closest object. When referring to Winnicott and others I use their original language for clarity (in this case "mother"), though the reader should understand the term more broadly as the person who is doing the mothering, whether they be male or female.
11. Similar conclusions were drawn by Bowlby in his development of attachment theory (Holmes, 1993).
12. While retaining Freud's notion of a libidinal drive-orientated id, the relational paradigm in which I work emphasises the object-seeking nature of unconscious desire over libido. Freud moves somewhat in this direction with his concept of eros (the life–love instinct) as having a binding capacity.
13. See above with regard to classical Freudian theory. Benjamin's theoretical advance is a development of Mahler's (1975) theory of separation and individuation, which implicitly sees the mother as an object through the eyes of the developing infant.
14. While this might seem a conventional sort of request at a speaking engagement, it is a rather odd one in the world of technology conferences, where audience members routinely tweet and blog *in medias res*.

Such "live blogging" as it is called, is often encouraged by organisers who give the event a hashtag (more on this in Chapter Six) so that members of the public not present at the event can follow along.

15. A different version of this chapter appeared first as a journal article entitled "TMI in the transference LOL: psychoanalytic reflections on Google, social networking, and 'virtual impingement'" in *Psychoanalysis, Culture and Society*, 17(2): 120–136. Although the original article has been altered a great deal, it remains highly clinically focused, which differentiates this chapter from others in the book, which are more directly applied outside the clinic.

16. Elsewhere (Balick, 2011a), I have written about how "cobbled together" identities are constructed at the level of personal narrative. The notion of an identity that is cobbled together from the virtual sources is a development of this idea.

17. Thomas's name and any identifying details have been changed. I am grateful to Thomas for his consenting to my use of this story; Thomas reviewed and commented on an earlier published version of this chapter.

18. The online world, in many ways, is boundary-less. The way that individuals manage its lack of boundaries (which then become that individual's choices) will be dependent on the characteristic ways in which they operate within their relational templates.

19. I will continue to stick closely to the case vignette here, as the themes developed in this case will ultimately enable us to apply them to online social networking in general. However, the way in which Thomas used the Internet as a tool to mediate his psychic state is clearly applicable to the wider population, and the mood in which such seeking occurs will be relevant to the experience in the process of online relational mediation.

20. Thomas reviewed the original version of this vignette before its first publication. He had very few corrections to make to it outside the fact that I had not included in the original draft his concern about my well-being. His request that I include it is testament to the meaning the potential harm to me had to him. It is also testament to the important intersubjective alliance we created between us.

21. I became aware of Lasdun's story through the extract published in *The Guardian*. A full account of his experience is available in his book *Give Me Everything You Have: On Being Stalked* (Lasdun, 2013b).

22. Despite the fact that an iPhone has the capacity to carry thousands of times more information than Voyager's phonograph, both Voyagers (I and II) are continuing to send back information to Earth despite being at the edge of the heliosphere and the furthest human-made objects to travel

so far in space; one is lucky if one's iPhone continues to process information at the end of a long day if it is not recharged.

23. Dunbar's number is an extrapolation of how human group sizes are likely to be based upon the size of the neocortex and

> can be interpreted as a direct cognitive limitation on the number of individuals with which an animal can simultaneously maintain relationships of sufficient depth that they can be relied upon to provide unstinting support when one of them is under attack. (Dunbar, 1998, p. 10)

Interestingly, Facebook users have an average of between 190 (Ugander, Karrer, Backstrom, & Marlow, 2011) and 229 friends (Hampton, Goulet, Rainie, & Purcell, 2011), not far off Dunbar's number, and not all friends are treated equally, as will be discussed in Chapter Four.

24. Narcissism, for Freud and later theorists, is a notoriously complex concept, partly due to the highly disputed nature of "primary narcissism". These complexities lie beyond the scope of this text, though the reader may wish to consult Hinshelwood (1991) to follow the development of narcissistic theory from Freud through Klein and the object relations school.

25. NPD is, in fact, obliquely included in the *ICD-10* under "Other Specific Personality Disorders" but does not include the comprehensive listing of characteristics found in the *DSM-IV-TR* (World Health Organization, 1992).

26. These phrases are rather problematic, since it is clear that another subject is never wholly "objectively" perceived.

27. "Cathexis" is one of the awkward usages that James Strachey, translator of the *Standard Edition*, applied to Freud's more prosaic terms in the original German. Bettelheim (1982) notes that Freud preferred simple terms and used the German word *Besetzung*, literally meaning "to occupy" (as in a military occupation). "Occupy" is more acceptable to Bettelheim, but he would also use "invest" (my chosen synonym) or "to fill" or "charge up". The use of "hyper-cathect" in this sentence may be more easily comprehended by thinking that each memory is "charged with feeling"; that certainly gives it a more human timbre.

28. One of these levels is most certainly how SNSs affect the way we deal with the ultimate loss of an object, the death of a friend or loved one. This function invites a whole series of questions about both the psychodynamic consequences of profiles of the dead remaining online and the growing legislative correlates with regard to who owns these profiles

after the original user has died, and what happens to them next. These problems are beyond the scope of this book.

29. Constitutional factors are also implicated here, in that frustration thresholds are likely to vary for different individuals, meaning the same mothering style (or, indeed, the same mother) may be good enough for one individual, but not another.

30. And, interestingly, in contrast to those who do not use the Internet at all, Facebook users are more than three times more likely to trust others (Hampton, Goulet, Rainie, & Purcell, 2011, p. 4).

31. Additionally, I maintain my own Social Media Research Facebook page, where I post most of the research I find in one place, and that can be accessed here: www.facebook.com/pages/Social-Media-Research/304715592897919.

32. These numbers are not mutually exclusive.

REFERENCES

Alexa (2012). www.alexa.com/topsites (accessed 4 December 2012).

American Psychiatric Association (2000). *Diagnostic and Statistical Manual of Mental Disorders: Fourth Edition: Text Revision* (*DSM-IV-TR*). Washington, DC: American Psychiatric Association.

Arehart-Treichel, J. (2011). Facebook can be useful—if you use common sense. *Psychiatric News, 36*(22): 5A.

Aron, L. (1996). *A Meeting of Minds: Mutuality in Psychoanalysis.* Hillsdale, NJ: Analytic Press.

Aron, L. (1999). The patient's experience of the analyst's subjectivity. In: S. A. Mitchell & L. Aron (Eds.), *Relational Psychoanalysis: The Emergence of a Tradition* (pp. 245–268). New York: Analytic Press.

Aron, L., & Harris, A. (2005). *Relational Psychoanalysis, Volume 2: Innovation and Expansion.* Hillsdale, NJ: Analytic Press.

Back, M., Stopfer, J., Vazire, S., Gaddis, S., Scmukle, S., Egloff, B., & Gosling, S. (2011). Facebook profiles reflect actual personality, not self-idealization. *Psychological Science, 21*(3): 372–374.

Backstrom, L., Bakshy, E., Kleinberg, J., Lento, T., Rosenn, I. (2011). Centre of Attention: how Facebook users allocate attention across friends. *Association for the Advancement of Artificial Intelligence.* http://misc.si.umich.edu/media/papers/attention.pdf (accessed 26 January 2013).

Bakshy, E. (2012). Rethinking information diversity in networks. Facebook. https://www.facebook.com/notes/facebook-data-team/rethinking-information-diversity-in-networks/10150503499618859 (accessed 26 January 2013).

Balick, A. (2008). The multiplicity of gender: an integrative psychoanalytic approach to theorising gender and sexual identities (Doctoral dissertation). Available from Albert Sloman Library: University of Essex. DXN121863.

Balick, A. (2011a). A very different kind of loss: memory, memorials, and 'cobbled together' sexual identities. *The Holocaust in History and Memory*, 4: 6–72.

Balick, A. (2011b). Speculating on sexual subjectivity: on the application and misapplication of postmodern discourse on the psychology of sexuality. *Psychology and Sexuality*, 2(1): 16–28.

Baraniuk, C. (2011). The quality of offline friendships. www.themachinestarts.com/read/2011-01-the-quality-of-offline-and-online-friendships (accessed 26 December 2012).

Barnett, E. (2011). Social network overuse 'breeds narcissism'. *Telegraph*, 9 August. www.telegraph.co.uk/technology/social-media/8689438/Social-network-overuse-breeds-narcissism.html (accessed 3 January 2013).

Baym, K. (2010). *Personal Connections in the Digital Age*. Cambridge, MA: Polity Press.

Benjamin, J. (1988). *The Bonds of Love: Psychoanalysis, Feminism, and the Problem of Domination*. New York: Pantheon.

Benjamin, J. (1990). An outline of intersubjectivity: the development of recognition. *Psychoanalytic Psychology*, 7S: 33–46.

Benjamin, J. (1995). *Like Subjects, Love Objects: Essays on Recognition and Sexual Difference*. New Haven, CT: Yale University Press.

Benjamin, J. (1998). *Shadow of the Other: Intersubjectivity and Gender in Psychoanalysis*. London: Routledge.

Benjamin, J. (2004). Beyond doer and done to: an intersubjective view of thirdness. *Psychoanalytic Quarterly*, 73S: 5–46.

Berne, E. (1964). *Games People Play: The Psychology of Human Relationships*. London & New York: Penguin.

Bettleheim, B. (1982). *Freud and Man's Soul*. London: Hogarth.

Bollas, C. (1987). *The Shadow of the Object: Psychoanalysis of the Unthought Known*. New York: Columbia University Press.

boyd, d. (2007). Why youth (heart) social network sites: the role of networked publics in teenage social life. In: D. Buckingham (Ed.),

MacArthur Foundation Series on Digital Learning: Youth, Identity, and Digital Media. Cambridge, MA: MIT Press.

boyd, d. (2008). Taken out of context: American teen sociality in networked publics (Doctoral dissertation). University of California-Berkely, School of Information.

boyd, d., & Ellison, N. B. (2007). Social network sites: definition, history, and scholarship. *Journal of Computer-Mediated Communication, 13*(1), article 11. http://jcmc.indiana.edu/vol13/issue1/boyd.ellison.html (accessed 25 September 2011).

Bryant, E., & Marmo, J. (2012). The rules of Facebook friendship: a two-stage examination of interaction rules in close, casual, and acquaintance friendships. *Journal of Social and Personal Relationships*, 1–23. DOI: 10.1177/0265407512443616.

Buffardi, L., & Campbell, W. (2008). Narcissism and social networking websites. *Personality and Social Psychology Bulletin, 34*: 1303–1314.

Burkeman, O. (2012). Facebook and Twitter: the art of unfriending or unfollowing people. www.guardian.co.uk/technology/2012/sep/14/unfollow-unfriend-on-facebook-twitter (accessed 7 November 2012).

Carr, N. (2010). *The Shallows: How the Internet Is Changing the Way We Think, Read and Remember*. New York: W. W. Norton.

Cascio, J. (2009). Get smarter. *The Atlantic*, July/August (accessed 14 November 2012).

Casement, P. (1985). *On Learning from the Patient*. London: Tavistock.

Cashdan, S. (1988). *Object Relations Therapy: Using the Relationship*. New York: W. W. Norton.

Christakis, N. (2010). Meet the new brain: same as the old brain. www.edge.org/q2010/q10_3.html#christakis (accessed 7 November 2012).

Clarke, B. (2009). Early adolescents' use of social networking sites to maintain friendship and explore identity: implications for policy. *Policy and Internet, 1*(1): 55–89.

Clarkson, P. (2003). *The Therapeutic Relationship* (2nd edn). London: Whurr.

Cooper, M. (2008). *Essential Research Findings in Counselling and Psychotherapy: The Facts Are Friendly*. London: Sage.

Cooper, S., & Levit, D. 1998 (2005). Old and new objects in Fairbairnian and American relational theory. In: L. Aron & A. Harris (Eds.), *Relational Psychoanalysis Volume 2: Innovation and Expansion* (pp. 51–74). Hillsdale NJ: Analytic Press.

Creeber, G., & Martin, R. (2009). *Digital Cultures: Understanding New Media*. Maidenhead: Open University Press.

Creswell, J. (2007). *Qualitative Inquiry and Research Design: Choosing Among the Five Approaches*. London: Sage.

Curk, P. (2007). From narcissism to mutual recognition. In: A. Gaitandidis & P. Curk (Eds.), *Narcissism: A Critical Reader* (pp. 71–92). London: Karnac.

Day, E. (2013). Interview. *The Observer*, 27 January 2013, p. 31.

Descartes, R. (1637). *Discourse on Method and The Meditations*, F. E. Sutcliffe (Trans.). Harmondsworth: Penguin, 1968.

Dreher, U. (2000). *Foundations for Conceptual Research in Psychoanalysis*, E. Ristle (Trans.). London: Karnac.

Duggan, M., & Brenner, J. (2013). The demographics of social media users—2012. *Pew Internet and American Life Project*, Washington DC, 14 February 2013. http://pewinternet.org/Reports/2013/Social-media-users.aspx (accessed 14 February 2013).

Dunbar, R. (1998). The social brain hypothesis. *Evolutionary Anthropology: Issues News and Reviews*, 6(5): 178–190.

Facebook (2011). Available from: www.facebook.com/press/info.php?statistics (accessed 22 September 2011).

Facebook (2012a). http://newsroom.fb.com/News/One-Billion-People-on-Facebook-1c9.aspx (accessed 15 October 2012).

Facebook (2012b). www.facebook.com/press/info.php?statistics (accessed 22 December 2012).

Fairbairn, W. R. D. (1944). Endopsychic structure considered in terms of object-relationships. *International Journal of Psychoanalysis*, 25: 70–92.

Firestone, L. (2012). Is social media to blame for the rise in Narcissism? *Psychology Today*, 29. www.psychologytoday.com/blog/compassion-matters/201211/is-social-media-blame-the-rise-in-narcissism (accessed 3 January 2013).

Fitzgerald, B. (2012). Most popular sites 2012: Alexa ranks the 500 most-visited websites. *Huffington Post* (accessed 3 October 2012).

Foresight Future Identities (2013). *Future Identities: Changing identities in the UK: The Next 10 Years*. London: The Government Office for Science.

Forrester, N. (2011). Social media: an epidemic of narcissism. *Huffington Post: Canada*, 12 December. www.huffingtonpost.ca/nicole-forrester/social-media—narcissism-_b_1128168.html (accessed 3 January 2013).

Freud, S. (1900a). *The Interpretation of Dreams. S.E., 3–4*. London: Hogarth.

Freud, S. (1907a). Delusions and dreams in Jensen's *Gradiva. S.E., 9*: 3–93. London: Hogarth.

Freud, S. (1910c). *Leonardo Da Vinci and a Memory of his Childhood. S.E., 11*: 59–138. London: Hogarth.

Freud, S. (1912e). Recommendations to physicians practising psycho-analysis. *S.E., 12*: 109–120. London: Hogarth.

Freud, S. (1914b). *The Moses of Michelangelo*. *S.E.*, *13*: 210–238. London: Hogarth.

Freud, S. (1915c). Instincts and their vicissitudes. *S.E.*, *14*: 161–215. London: Hogarth.

Freud, S. (1915e). The unconscious. *S.E.*, *14*: 166–204. London: Hogarth.

Freud, S. (1917e). Mourning and melancholia. *S.E.*, *14*: 239–258. London: Hogarth.

Freud, S. (1923b). *The Ego and the Id*. *S.E.*, *19*: 3–39. London: Hogarth.

Freud, S. (1925a). A note on the mystic writing pad. *S.E.*, *19*: 227–232. London: Hogarth.

Freud, S. (1939a). *Moses and Monotheism*. *S.E.*, *23*: 3–137. London: Hogarth.

Frosh, S. (2006). Melancholy without the other. *Studies in Gender and Sexuality*, *7*(4): 363–378.

Frosh, S. (2010). *Psychoanalysis Outside the Clinic: Interventions in Psychosocial Studies*. London: Palgrave.

Gabbard, G. (2001). Cyberpassion: e-rotic transference on the Internet. *Psychoanalytic Quarterly*, *70*: 719–737.

Gibbs, P. (2007). Reality in cyberspace: analysands' use of the Internet and ordinary everyday psychosis. *Psychoanalytic Review*, *94*: 11–38.

Goffman, E. (1955). One face-work: an analysis of ritual elements in social interaction. *Psychiatry*, *15*(4): 451–463.

Goldacre, B. (2009). *Bad Science*. London: Harper Perrenial.

Google (2012). The New Multi-screen World: understanding cross-platform consumer behaviour, August 2012. Available from: www.google.com/think/research-studies/the-new-multi-screen-world-study.html (accessed 1 August 2013).

Gorden, C. (2010). Who's afraid of Google? In: J. Petrucelli (Ed.), *Knowing, Not-Knowing & . . . Sort-of-Knowing: Psychoanalysis and the Experience of Uncertainty* (pp. 315–324). London: Karnac.

Görzig, A. (2011). Who bullies and who is bullied online? *EU Kids Online*. Available from: www2.lse.ac.uk/media@lse/research/EUKids Online/EU%20Kids%20Online%20reports.aspx (accessed 27 January 2012).

Greenberg, J., & Mitchell, S. A. (1983). *Object Relations in Psychoanalytic Theory*. Cambridge, MA: Harvard University Press.

Greene, R. (2012). Like? *Intelligent Life*, May/June: 72–77.

Greif, D. (2011). The revitalization of psychoanalysis: antidote to 'instant culture'. Paper given at International Association of Relational Psychoanalysis and Psychotherapy: Changing Psychoanalysis for a Changing Society. Madrid: 29 June to 2 July.

Hampton, K., Goulet, L. S., Rainie, L., & Purcell, K. (2011). *Social Networking Sites and our Lives: How People's Trust, Personal Relationships, and Civic and Political Involvement Are Connected to Their Use of Social Networking Sites and Other Technologies.* Washington, DC: Pew Research Centre.

Hampton, K., Sessions, L., Her, E. J., & Rainie, L. (2009). *Social Isolation and New Technology: How the Internet and Mobile Phones Impact Americans' Social Networks.* Washington, DC: Pew Research Centre.

Hartman, S. (2011). Reality 2.0: when loss is lost. *Psychoanalytic Dialogues, 21*(4): 468–482.

Hawthorne, N. (1850). *The Scarlet Letter.* Kindle edition.

Heimann, P. (1950). On counter-transference. *International Journal of Psychoanalysis, 31*: 81–84.

Hinshelwood, R. D. (1991). *A Dictionary of Kleinian Thought.* London: Free Association Books.

Hollway, W., & Jefferson, T. (2010). *Doing Qualitative Research Differently: Free Association, Narrative and the Interview Method.* London: Sage.

Holmes, J. (1993). *John Bowlby and Attachment Theory.* London: Routledge.

Jacobs, M. (1998). *The Presenting Past; The Core of Psychodynamic Counselling and Therapy.* Buckingham: Open University Press.

Johnson, S. (1987). *Humanising the Narcissistic Style.* New York: W. W. Norton.

Johnson, S. (1994). *Character Styles.* New York: W. W. Norton.

Jung, C. G. (1966). *Two Essays on Analytical Psychology*, R. F. C. Hull (Trans.). Princeton, NJ: Princeton University Press.

Kirkpatrick, D. (2010). *The Facebook Effect: The Inside Story of the Company That Is Connecting the World.* Kindle Version: Virgin.

Kirkpatrick, M. (2010). Google CEO Schmidt: people aren't ready for the technology revolution. http://readwrite.com/2010/08/04/google_ceo_schmidt_people_arent_ready_for_the_tech (accessed 22 December 2012).

Klein, M. (1935). A contribution to the psychogenesis of manic-depressive states. *International Journal of Psychoanalysis, 16*: 145–174.

Klein, M. (1946). *Envy and Gratitude and Other Works 1946–1963.* London: Vintage. 1988.

Kolmes, K. (2012). Articles for clinicians using social media. http://drkkolmes.com/for-clinicians/articles/#social%20media%20policy (accessed 10 February 2012).

Kolmes, K., Nagel, D., & Anthony, K. (2011). An ethical framework for the use of social media by mental health professionals. *Tilt Magazine*, 3 January. www.issuu.com/onlinetherapyinstitute/docs/issue3 (accessed 19 February 2013).

Kozinets, R. (2010). *Nethnography: Doing Ethnographic Research Online.* London: Sage.

Kranzberg, M. (1986). Technology and history: Kranzberg's laws. *Technology and Culture, 27*(3). 544–560.

Kraut, R., Patterson, M., Lundmark, V., Kisler, S., Mukopadhyay, T., & Scherlis, W. (1998). Internet paradox. A social technology that reduces social involvement and psychological well-being? *American Psychology, 53*(9): 1017–1031.

Kühn, S., Romanowksi, A., Schilling, C., Lorenz, R., Mörsen, C., Seirferth, N., Banaschewski, T., Barbot, A., Barker, G. J., Büchel, C., Conrond, P. J., Dalley, J. W., Flor, H., Garavan, H., Ittermann, B., Mann, K., Martinot, J. L., Paus, T., Rietschel, M., Smolka, M. N., Strölhe, A., Walaszek, B., Schumann, G., Heinz, A., Gallinat, J., & The IMAGEN Consortium (2011). The neural basis of video gaming. *Translational Psychiatry, 1*(53): 1–5.

Lampe, C., Ellison, N., & Steinfield, C. (2006). A Face(book) in the crowd: social searching vs social browsing. Paper presented at the 20th Anniversary Conference on Computer Supported Cooperative Work, New York.

Lanier, J. (2011). *You Are Not a Gadget.* London: Penguin.

Laplanche, J., & Pontalis, J. (1988). *The Language of Psychoanalysis.* London: Karnac.

Lasch, C. (1979). *The Culture of Narcissism: American Life in an Age of Diminishing Expectations.* London: W. W. Norton.

Lasdun, J. (2013a). I will ruin him. *Guardian Weekend Magazine,* 2 February 2013, pp. 26–33.

Lasdun, J. (2013b). *Give Me Everything You Have: On Being Stalked.* London: Jonathan Cape.

Lingiardi, V. (2008). Playing with unreality: transference and computer. *International Journal of Psychoanalysis, 89*: 111–126.

Lingiardi, V. (2011). Realities in dialogue: commentary on paper by Stephen Hartman. *Psychoanaltyic Dialogues, 21*(4): 483–495.

Loewenthal, D., & Snell, R. (2003). *Post-modernism for Psychotherapists: A Critical Reader.* Hove: Taylor and Francis.

Lustig, R. (2012). *Fat Chance: A Bitter Truth about Sugar.* London: Fourth Estate.

Lyotard, J.-F. (1984). *The Postmodern Condition: A Report on Knowledge.* Manchester: Manchester University Press.

Mahler, M. (1975). *The Psychological Birth of the Infant.* New York: Basic Books.

Malater, E. (2007a). Introduction: special issue on the Internet. *Psychoanalytic Review*, 94: 3–6.

Malater, E. (2007b). Caught in the web: patient, therapist, email, and the Internet. *Psychoanalytic Review*, 94: 151–168.

Marche, S. (2012). Is Facebook making us lonely? *The Atlantic*, May. www. theatlantic.com/magazine/archive/2012/05/is-facebook-making-us-lonely/8930/# (accessed 17 April 2012).

Marlow, C. (2009). Maintained relationships on Facebook. www.facebook.com/note.php?note_id=55257228858 (accessed 2 January 2012).

Maroda, K. (2004). *The Power of Countertransference: Innovations in Analytic Technique*. Hillsdale, NJ: Analytic Press.

Marshall, T. (2012). Facebook surveillance of former romantic partners: associations with postbreakup recovery and personal growth. *Cyberpsychology, Behavior, and Social Networking*, 15(10). DOI: 10.1089/cyber.201.0125.

McCartney, M. (2012). How much of a social media profile can doctors have? *British Medical Journal*, 23 January: 344: e440.

McLuhan, M. (1964). *Understanding Media*. New York: Routledge, 2001.

Meikle, J. (2012). Twitter is harder to resist than cigarettes and alcohol, study finds. *Guardian*. Available from: www.guardian.co.uk/technology/2012/feb/03/twitter-resist-cigarettes-alcohol-study?CMP=twt_gu (accessed 22 March 2012).

Midgely, N. (2006). The inseparable bond between cure and research: clinical case study as a method of psychoanalytic inquiry. *Journal of Child Psychotherapy*, 32(2): 122–147.

Mitchell, S. (1988). *Relational Concepts in Psychoanalysis: An Integration*. Cambridge, MA: Harvard University Press.

Mitchell, S. (1993). *Hope and Dread in Psychoanalysis*. New York: Basic Books.

Mitchell, S., & Aron, L. (1999). *Relational Psychoanalysis: The Emergence of a Tradition*. New York: Analytic Press.

Mitchell, S., & Black, M. (1995). *Freud and Beyond: A History of Modern Psychoanalytic Thought*. New York: Basic Books.

Mitchell, S., & Greenberg, J. (1983). *Object Relations in Psychoanalytic Theory*. Cambridge, MA: Harvard University Press.

Morozov, E. (2011). *The Net Delusion: How Not To Liberate the World*. London: Allen Lane.

Nadkarni, A., & Hofmann, S. (2012). Why do people use Facebook? *Personality and Individual Differences*, 52: 243–249.

Naughton, J. (2012a). *From Gutenberg to Zuckerberg; What You Really Need To Know about the Internet*. London: Quercus.

Naughton, J. (2012b). Will big business and politicians end up controlling the free-thinking net? *Observer*, 23 December.

Neilsen (2012). State of the media: social media report. The Neilson Company. http://blog.nielsen.com/nielsenwire/social/2012/ (accessed 1 March 2013).

Ofcom (2008). *Social Networking: A Quantitative and Qualitative Research Report into Attitudes, Behaviours and Use*. London: Office of Communications (Ofcom).

Ofcom (2011). A nation addicted to smartphones. http://consumers.ofcom.org.uk/2011/08/a-nation-addicted-to-smartphones/ (accessed 7 November 2012).

Ogden, T. (1999). The analytic third: working with intersubjective clinical facts. In: S. Mitchell & L. Aron, L. (Eds.), *Relational Psychoanalysis: The Emergence of a Tradition* (pp. 459–492). Hillsdale, NJ: Analytic Press.

Ogden, T. (2004). The analytic third: implications for psychoanalytic theory and technique. *Psychoanalytic Quarterly, 73*: 167–195.

O'Keefe, G., & Clarke-Pearson, K. (2011). Clinical report—the impact of social media on children, adolescents, and families. *Pediatrics, 27*(4): 800–804. http://pediatrics.aappublications.org/content/early/2011/03/28/peds.2011–0054.abstract (accessed 30 March 2012).

Olweus, D. (1993). *Bullying at School: What We Know and What We Can Do*. Oxford: Blackwell.

Ophir, E., Nass, C., & Wagner, A. (2009). Cognitive control in media multitaskers. *Proceedings of the National Academy of Sciences, 106*: 15583–15587.

Orbach, S. (2002). *On Eating: Change Your Eating, Change Your Life*. London: Penguin.

Orbach, S. (2006). *Fat is a Feminist Issue*. London: Arrow.

Orbach, S. (2009). *Bodies*. London: Profile.

Palfrey, J., & Gasser, U. (2008). *Born Digital: Understanding the First Generation of Digital Natives*. New York: Basic Books.

Pearse, D. (2012). Facebook's 'dark side': study finds link to socially aggressive narcissism. *Guardian*, 17 March. www.guardian.co.uk/technology/2012/mar/17/facebook-dark-side-study-aggressive-narcissism (accessed 3 January 2013).

Pepitone, J. (2012). Facebook trading sets record IPO volume. CNN MONEY: http://money.cnn.com/2012/05/18/technology/facebook-ipo-trading/index.htm (accessed 3 October 2012).

Quinodoz, J. M. (2004). *Reading Freud: A Chronological Exploration of Freud's Writings*, D. Alcorn (Trans.). London: Routledge.

Rainie, L., Smith, A., & Duggan, M. (2013). Coming and going on Facebook. *Pew Internet and American Life Project*, Washington DC, 5 February 2013. http://pewinternet.org/~/media//Files/Reports/2013/PIP_Coming_and_going_on_facebook.pdf (accessed 15 February 2013).

Riesman, D., Glazer, N., & Denny, R. (1950). *The Lonely Crowd: A Study of Changing American Character.* New Haven, CT: Yale University Press, 2001.

Ronningstam, E. (2005). *Identifying and Understanding the Narcissistic Personality.* Oxford: Oxford University Press.

Rosen, L. (2011). How media distorts scientific results. *Psychology Today*, 27 August. www.psychologytoday.com/blog/rewired-the-psychology-technology/201108/how-media-distorts-scientific-results (accessed 3 January 2013).

Roughton, R. (1995). Action and acting out. In: B. Moore & B. Fine (Eds.), *Psychoanalysis: The Major Concepts* (pp. 130–145). New Haven, CT: Yale University Press.

Rumsfeld, D. (2002). DoD news briefing—Secretary Rumsfeld and Gen. Myters. News Transcript, 12 February 2002. www.defense.gov/transcripts/transcript.aspx?transcriptid=2636 (accessed 5 May 2013).

Ryan, T., & Xenos, S. (2011). Who uses Facebook? An investigation into the relationship between the Big Five, shyness, narcissism, loneliness, and Facebook usage. *Computers in Human Behavior, 27*: 1658–1664.

Samuels, A. (1985). *Jung and the Post-Jungians.* New York: Routledge.

Samuels, A. (2013). Personal communication.

Sand, S. (2007). Future considerations: interactive identities and the interactive self. *Psychoanalytic Review, 94*: 83–97.

Seidman, S. (1993). Identity and politics in a "postmodern" gay culture. In: W. Michael (Ed.), *Fear of a Queer Planet: Queer Politics and Social Theory* (pp. 105–142). Minneapolis, MN: University of Minnesota Press.

Seligman, A. (2009). Well connected? The biological implications of social networking. *The Biologist, 56*(1): 14–20.

Seligman, S. (2011). Psychoanalytic ideals, new technologies, and the expropriations of the corporate self: commentary on paper by Stephen Hartman. *Psychoanalytic Dialogues, 21*(4): 496–507.

Short, J., Bohn, R., & Baru, C. (2011). How much information? 2010: report on enterprise server information. University of California, San Diego. http://hmi.ucsd.edu/pdf/HMI_2010_EnterpriseReport_Jan_2011.pdf (accessed 22 December 2012).

Slavin, M., & Kriegman, D. (1998). Why the analyst needs to change: toward a theory of conflict, negotiation, and mutual influence in the therapeutic process. In: L Aron & A. Harris (Eds.), *Relational Psychoanalysis, Volume 2: Innovation and Expansion* (pp. 75–120). Hillsdale, NJ: Analytic Press, 2005.

Slochower, J. (2005). Holding: something old and something new. In: L. Aron & A. Harris (Eds.), *Relational Psychoanalysis, Volume 2: Innovation and Expansion* (pp. 29–49). Hillsdale, NJ: Analytic Press.

Small, G. W., Moody, T. D., Siddarth, P., & Bookheimer, S. Y. (2009). Your brain on Google: patterns of cerebral activation during internet searching. *American Journal of Geriatric Psychiatry, 17*(2): 116–126.

Smith, A., & Brenner, J. (2012). Twitter use 2012. *Pew Internet and American Life Project.* Washington DC: Pew Research Centre.

Smith, P., Mahdavi, J., Carvalho, M., Fisher, S., Russell, S., & Tippett, N. (2008). Cyberbullying: its nature and impact in secondary school pupils. *Journal of Child Psychology and Psychiatry, 49*(4): 376–385.

Solis, B. (2012). Facebook: over 1 billion served—plus interesting stats. www.briansolis.com/2012/10/facebook-over-1-billion-served-plus-interesting-stats/ (accessed 22 December 2012).

Stenovec, T. (2011). Myspace history: a timeline of the social network's biggest moments. *Huffington Post.* Available from: www.huffington-post.com/2011/06/29/myspace-history-timeline_n_887059.html#s299496&title=August_2003_Myspace (accessed 22 September 2011).

Stone, L. (2012). Continuous partial attention. http://lindastone.net/qa/continuous-partial-attention/ (accessed 7 November 2012).

Sturken, M., & Thomas, D. (2004). Introduction: technological visions and rhetoric of the new. In: M. Sturken, D. Thomas, & S. J. Ball-Rokeach (Eds.), *Technological Visions: The Hopes and Fears that Shape New Technologies* (pp. 1–18). Philadelphia, PA: Temple University Press.

Swift, M. (2012). Making new connections. *Denver Post*, 23 January, p. 15A.

Thaler, R., & Sunstein, C. (2008). *Nudge: Improving Decisions about Health, Wealth, and Happiness.* New Haven, CT: Yale University Press.

The Economist (2011). Sharing the power of 2012, 17 November. www.economist.com/node/21537000 (accessed 21 December 2012).

The Economist (2012). Floating Facebook: the value of friendship, 4 February.

They Might Be Giants (1990). *Birdhouse in Your Soul.* TMBG Music (BMI).

Tobak, S. (2012). Social networks and the narcissism epidemic. *CBS Money Watch*, 29 August. www.cbsnews.com/8301–505125_162–57502035/social-networks-and-the-narcissism-epidemic/ (accessed 3 January 2013).

Turkle, S. (2004). Whither psychoanalysis in computer culture. *Psychoanalytic Psychology, 21*: 16–30.

Turkle, S. (2011). *Alone Together: Why We Expect More from Technology and Less from Each Other*. New York: Basic Books.

Ugander, J., Karrer, B., Backstrom, L., & Marlow, C. (2011). The anatomy of the Facebook social graph. http://arxiv.org/pdf/1111.4503v1.pdf (accessed 2 January 2013).

Ultima, M., Escola, L., Instkirveli, F., Grammont, M., Caruana, A., Gallese, V., & Rizzolatti, G. (2008). When pliers become fingers in the monkey motor system. *Proceedings of the National Academy of Sciences, 10*(5/6): 2209–2013.

Valenzuela, S., Park, N., & Kee, K. (2009). Is there social capital in a social network site?: Facebook use and college students' life satisfaction, trust, and participation. *Journal of Computer-Mediated Communication, 14*: 875–901.

Van Grove, J. (2013). Why teens are tiring of Facebook. CNET News: http://news.cnet.com/8301–1023_3–57572154–93/why-teens-are-tiring-of-facebook/ (accessed 2 March 2013).

Vanderbilt, T. (2013). The future of search. *Wired Magazine*, January: 104–111.

Wilcox, K., & Stephen, A. (2012). Are close friends the enemy? Online social networks, self esteem, and self control. *Journal of Consumer Research, 40*. DOI: 10.1086/668794.

Winnicott, D. W. (1956). On transference. *International Journal of Psychoanalysis, 37*: 386–388.

Winnicott, D. W. (1960). The theory of the parent–infant relationship. *International Journal of Psychoanalysis, 41*: 585–595.

Winnicott, D. W. (1964). *The Child, the Family and the Outside World*. London: Penguin.

Winnicott, D. W. (1969). The use of an object. *International Journal of Psychoanalysis, 50*: 711–716.

Winnicott, D. W. (1971). *Playing and Reality*. London: Tavistock.

Winnicott, D. W. (1982a). Ego distortion in terms of true and false self. In: J. Sutherland (Ed.), *The Maturational Processes and the Facilitating Environment: Studies in the Theory of Emotional Development* (pp. 140–152). London: Hogarth Press.

Winnicott, D. W. (1982b). From dependence towards independence in the development of the individual. In: J. Sutherland (Ed.), *The Maturational Processes and the Facilitating Environment: Studies in theTheory of Emotional Development* (pp. 83–92). London: Hogarth Press.

Winnicott, D. W. (1982c). The capacity to be alone. In: J. Sutherland (Ed.), *The Maturational Processes and the Facilitating Environment: Studies in the Theory of Emotional Development* (pp. 29–36). London: Hogarth Press.

Winnicott, D. W. (1986). Transitional objects and transitional phenomena: a study of the first not-me possession. In: P. Buckly (Ed.), *Essential Papers on Object Relations* (pp. 254–271). New York: New York University Press.

Wolak, J., Mitchell, K., & Finkelhor, D. (2003). Escaping or connecting? Characteristics of youth who form close online relationships. *Journal of Adolescence, 26*: 105–119.

Woods, J. (2013). Child abuse on a massive scale: the harm being done by unrestricted Internet pornography. Paper given at "Virtual adolescence: the Internet, social networking and video games", 9 February 2013, London, University College London.

World Health Organization (1992). *International Classifications of Mental and Behavioural Disorders: Clinical Descriptions and Diagnostic Guidelines (ICD-10)*. Geneva: World Health Organization.

INDEX